The Apocalypse Project

by Briandaniel Oglesby

Uproar Theatrics

LICENSING & PRODUCTION INQUIRIES
Uproar Theatrics, LLC.
hello@uproartheatrics.com | www.UproarTheatrics.com

About The Apocalypse Project

I originally wrote this play in the last few months of 2019. I write many of my plays with a group of young collaborators, and this version is built around the people who were in the room. I invite you to tailor this play to your ensemble: **all roles can be played by any gender.** This flexibility is imbedded into the play itself. More details below.

This is a play about the current moment expressed through an alternate reality where adults have vanished leaving pain and rubble; the young people have to put the pieces together in a world they did not create. Because that is the charge every generation leaves for the next - to fix the mistakes of the past while making new mistakes. The challenge is to make a play that's not a trudge toward death, that's not consumed with grief for the people who are gone, but finds the joy and hope while in the darkness. To make a play that's harrowing yet gleeful. Dark and yet fun, serious and glib. To fill it with trash and decay, but to have the green poking through.

This play was originally created with and for the students of Skybridge Academy (now Appamada School).

The cast consisted of
Trinity Bobo (T)
Nicholas Dussere (Lor)
Collin Beck (Scrapper)
Jacob Gantenbein (Mr. Avers)
Percy Young (Shane)
Griffin Wilson (Collin Beck and Mean Math Dude)
Ethan Hennenhoefer (Adam, Chris, Ensemble)
Dorian "Zev" Kweller (Ozli, The Headmaster, Ensemble)
Ezra Wilson (Bolt, Ensemble)

Torin Ginty (DJ, Johnny B, Ensemble)

Instructions on Casting / Gender

I originally wrote this for a group that had two girls and eight boys, and who were a mix of cis and trans. I never pre-cast, so every part was gender neutral in the writing process. The romantic relationship was written without pre-assigning the characters' genders, but works best as queer. For clarity, I have left the pronouns from the original casting in place. Please adjust these to your needs.

Time and Setting

We set The Disappearance to be February 14, 2020, two months after the performances of the play. Music and cultural products that were popular when we produced the play, like Old Town Road and Fortnite, would be the last bits of culture preserved in the consciousness of the characters. For future production, you have two options:

1. to keep The Disappearance on the original date and assume that you're creating an alternative history.
2. or to set The Disappearance a couple months after your production.

If you set it a couple months after your production, please adjust references to fit whatever is popular at the time. I'll go into this a bit more in the Postscript Letter.

CHARACTERS
This was initially written for a cast of ten actors for a tiny black box theatre. For the original doubling, read the postscript.

Altierra

The Expelled
T — Our guide. T is 14. T wants to be a Youtuber. Youtube may be dead, but that doesn't stop T. Having always been kept safe by others, T craves adventure.

LOR — Lor is 19. Asthmatic. Worrier, but resigned to the fate.

SCRAPPER — Lor's sibling. Scrapper runs hot, and is always up to start a fight. Wants nothing more than to go out and DO SOMETHING.

Mr. AVERS — Bombastic traveler. Mr. Avers has seen the country.

SHANE — Hotheaded Shane doesn't think much of humanity.

The Others of Altierra
BOLT — Leader of the Altierra Compound, though sees self as more of a facilitator. Optimistic about the future.

MEAN MATH DUDE— In charge of water at Altierra

ADAM — A part of the Altierra compound

OZLI — A young member of Altierra.

DJ — Focuses on weapons. Liked Ren faires in the old days.

St. Mikey's
BOOTLICKER — Henchperson for the Headmaster.

BRAT — Another henchperson for The Headmaster.

THE HEADMASTER — Dictator of St Mikey's.

"In time the murky skies would clear up and the rains would wash the scum from the rivers and lakes. The tall buildings would come tumbling down and the freeways would crumble away. And in time the green growth would wind its way up through the rubble. But the Wump World would never be quite the same."
- *Wump World*, Bill Peet

"It's a small world, after all"
- Disney Proverb

For: Collin, Ezra, Nicholas, Griffin, Percy, Ethan, Dorian, Trinity, Torin, Jacob, Roman, Claire, and Sam.

The Road

COLLIN BECK — Wild-eyed. Looks young for his age. A bit intense.

YOUNG ADULT — 21-year old scavenger

SECOND YOUNG ADULT — 21-year-old scavenger

THE FERAL CHILD — Wears a baseball cap. Seen in Prologue AND end of Act 1.

THE CITIZEN — Really loves what Lor does.

SAD DISNEYKID — Wears a Disney-inspired shirt that's too small

CHRIS — Lor and Scrapper's cousin. A bro. Used to resent older people, but loved what he inherited when they left.

JOHNNY B — Canadian EMT.

MOM and DAD — Lor's imaginary parents at Sad Disneyland.

Ensemble Parts

Additional Altierra kids, others in the battle at St. Mikey's, mourners at the memorial, audience in the Oregon show, costumed members of Sad Disneyland, New York musical theatre kids, and Firestarters.

Prologue. February 14, 2023
As the audience enters

*In a field of concrete. A lone figure around a
fire. If you weren't looking too hard, you could
mistake this figure for a kid on a camping trip.
Now, about that fire - look closely, it's fueled by
bits of furniture, broken chairs, a couple old
books. There could even be a grill, one that is
not barbecue, but birdcage or something similar.
It's an improvised set up. Scrounged. It's almost
a   parody of a camping trip. The kid is fiddling
with aluminum foil. He wears a ragged baseball
cap. Another young person joins the kid. This
one is slightly older - a young adult. He carries
a backpack.*

KID

Hey.

YOUNG ADULT

Hey.

*They dab. The YOUNG ADULT takes a radio
out of his bag. He snatches the foil from the kid.
The kid sticks his tongue out at him. The
YOUNG ADULT gives him a look.
The YOUNG ADULT fashions the foil into an
antennae.
A SECOND YOUNG ADULT enters. This one
carries a heavy, overloaded pack.
The SECOND YOUNG ADULT drops this in a
heap. They dab.*

KID

Hey.

YOUNG ADULT

Hey.

SECOND YOUNG ADULT

Hey.

> *The KID goes to look into the pack and is pushed away.*

KID

Hey!

SECOND YOUNG ADULT

Dude.

> *The SECOND YOUNG ADULT reaches into the pack and tosses the YOUNG ADULT a beer[1].*

KID

Yo!

SECOND YOUNG ADULT

Pft. Ain't old 'nough.

YOUNG ADULT

Gotta be 21.

---

[1] We went with White Claw. They're easy to fake and White Claw says 2019/2020.

                    KID

Who gonna care? You?

              SECOND YOUNG ADULT

21.

          The KID lunges for it anyway.

                YOUNG ADULT

Hey.

              SECOND YOUNG ADULT

Heh. Fine.

          The KID drinks.
          Ugh. Nasty. Like this-beer-is-three-years-old
          nasty.

                    KID

NASTY.

              SECOND YOUNG ADULT

It's old.

          This is probably when the play starts. Like this is
          when the audience hushes and house lights dim
          and everyone realizes things are starting.

                YOUNG ADULT

You. You find any? You, hey, did you?

              SECONG YOUNG ADULT

Ask nicely.

YOUNG ADULT

Screw you.

SECOND YOUNG ADULT

There we go.

*SECOND YOUNG ADULT tosses YOUNG
ADULT a pack of batteries.*

SECOND YOUNG ADULT

Call me Batt-Man.

YOUNG ADULT

Whatever.

*YOUNG ADULT puts these batteries into the
radio.*

SECOND YOUNG ADULT

Don't blame me if they're dead.

*They turn on the radio.
Static*

KID

Told you.

YOUNG ADULT

Shut up.

*Static
Then…. music.
A beat as they realize what this means. Then
excitement.*

YOUNG ADULT

Ha!

SECOND YOUNG ADULT

Someone got a station running. Someone got power,
someone got a station running!

YOUNG ADULT

What did I tell you, what did I tell you?

SECOND YOUNG ADULT

Turn it up.

> *They turn it up high, loud, their excitement*
> *flooding through and allowing them to be*
> *ridiculous.*
> *Holy crap this is awesome this is awesome this*
> *is so awesome*
> *Every rusty dance move from back when the*
> *world was still together explodes into their*
> *revelry.*
> *And then... Time seems to slow. A strobe*
> *flashing.*
> *There's a rattle. A hiss. It's otherworldly, but not*
> *exactly alien.*
> *A sudden intense blinding light.*
> *Blackout.*
> *Then - the firelight returns.*
> *The two YOUNG ADULTS have vanished. The*
> *KID is still dancing.*
> *The radio breaks into static again. KID looks*
> *around.*

                              KID

Hello? Hello?
                    (This is not funny.)
Not again.

                    Static.
                    END of SCENE

Act 1
ONE - THE HOMESTEAD
The Apocalypse Project - 2024 - March

*[OPTIONAL: A soundscape brings us to a year
later: static fades into songs from 2019, and this
nostalgia carries us into more serious stuff: bits
and pieces of news and culture from around that
time: CNN, war, impeachment, climate change.
Hurricanes. Fire. Noise and chaos. A blip cuts
through - it fizzles like firecrackers into a pure
tone.]
The sounds of a working farm.
A compound somewhere in Texas - in the
outskirts of the outskirts of Austin.
And then - T is in front of a well-decorated hutch
with a multi-plug, which is plugged into a
battery, which is attached to a solar panel.
Most of the outlets are in use - each one labeled:
"Kitchen," "Water pump," etc. But there is one
empty one labeled "For Us" from which T has
just unplugged her phone.
T turns on her phone.
Behind and around T, we see the young people
who populate the Altierra compound. They are
working. Everyone has something to do.*

T

It works.
		(to someone off camera.)
I told you it would work.
		*(Answer from the Altierra kid: "It's your power,
		man.")*
What's up, cultural scavengers of future-times? …
To those who may find this.

1

*(someone passes by, carrying some equipment. T
gets self-conscious, but then continues)*

T (CONT)

What you need to know is that on February 14, 2020, four
years ago, every person over the age of 20 in the whole
world disappeared.

We took a collective double-blink, and in the infinite second
our eyes shut, the adults vanished. No trace. No dust. No
goodbyes.

You can call me "T."

*(SCRAPPER goes to the rainwater collection
and fills a pot)*

Yeah. Just that. Because it's a — we call ourselves what we
want. Names remind us of…

(this hurts a bit, but T covers it up.)

Yeah. Why not? You know, I can go by anything I want. We
all do.

And I uh.

(T recovers)

And, I'm coming at you from the Altierra Compound on this
day, March 1, 2024.

Today I'm 14.

And so today, this day, I make my first entry into The
Apocalypse Project.

(T hums a bit of intro music. It's dorky.)

Uh. Sometimes humor helps.

*LOR is coughing. SCRAPPER gets him water.
MEAN MATH DUDE, who monitors water,
snaps at him.*

MATH (to SCRAPPER).

Hey! What part of "drought" don't you understand,
Scrapper?

SCRAPPER

It's for my brother.

MATH

He can get his own ration.

SCRAPPER

He's having asthma —

MATH

Are his legs broken?? No, no they are not.

BOLT, the clipboard-wielding leader, calls out.

BOLT

Everything PC over there y'all?

LOR

Don't use me as an excuse, numbskull. I'm fine.

SCRAPPER

Die then, I don't care.

BOLT

What do we need?

T

A time out!

A blink.

T

It's a joke. Hah. Humor?
(back to the video)
So … With no one manning the grid, and anyone with a
password gallivanting through dimension X or wherever, we
had electricity for like fifteen minutes.

BOLT

You're making a video about the Disappearance?

LOR

Of course she is.

BOLT

Cool.

T

It didn't help that Yet Another Storm of the Century was
pummeling us at the time —

BOLT addresses the camera.

BOLT

That storm was a blessing.
It meant that a bunch of them were mercifully stuck at
Austin-Bergstrom International Airport instead of hanging
midair on Southwest 242 to Denver when the pilot raptured.

T

Okay.
Some things spun down gracefully.
Some things ended with a bang.
You could hear the transformers exploding like fireworks.
Pop pop pop.

Houston is still on fire, belching toxic smoke that's turning much of the gulf and Louisiana into acid soup. I heard that it will be on fire for a hundred years.

We had plenty of cars, but only so much gas, and what we had went bad after a little while.

And then there were the nuke plants, captain-less oil tankers, subs adrift like pills of nuclear poison.

> *Two of the Altierra kids are trying to remember Old Town Road. They give T a look as she passes by them.*

T

Even with all that, we thought we could, uh, rebuild.

19 year-olds saw their odometers turn over to 20, then 21, 22...

Then, a year ago, it happened a second time.

MATH

That's when things got bad.

T

Or so I've heard.

The Altierra compound has been my home since Day Zero.

Say, "Hi," Altierra!

ALTIERRA KIDS greet the camera.

SHANE

That is so dumb. You are so dumb.

BOLT

Language.

T

We got - greenhouses, vegetable gardens, rainwater collection. Craft shop. Sick-space. The Private Room, if you need to cry. And most important of all, our friend the solar panel.

I get 30 minutes to plug whatever I want.

...

We think we have two years before it happens again. I'll be 16.

Lor, there, will be 20. If he makes it that long.

Scrapper will be 17.

MATH

SCRAPPER!

T

If *he* makes it that long.

MATH

You got a *job*. Do it.

T
(pointing at different people)

16, 19, 13 — Shane 21

We all pitch in at Altierra, but then we got the thing we do that's *ours*.

I'm in charge of The Library. I make two copies of everything.

(The Library is a big binder full of papers - T
shows it to the camera)

How to make a water filter.

How to fix a bike chain.

The Heimlich.

How to tourniquet a wound.

Maps.

*BOLT rings a bell. Everyone in the compound
gathers.*

                                       .

                           T

And once a week we hold an argument circle where we fight
about what we think happened.

                       BOLT

Alright my dudes! You know the rules. We're going to have
a *healthy* argument here. One minute, go!

                      ADAM

We should use the talking stick.

              THE ARGUMENT CIRCLE
              *(Note: actors pick an argument and develop this
              to fit in the allotted time. Let these arguments be
              consistent with the character's POV. If there are
              more actors than arguments, the actor should
              invent their own argument consistent with their
              character's point of view.)*

              *These are said simultaneously.
              People are talking all at once but barely
              listening.
              This is what it means to be part of Altierra.*

              THE ALIEN ARGUMENT

It's the only thing that makes sense. It's too specific and yet
arbitrary, so an extraterrestrial intelligence must be at work. I
don't know why. Remember alien movies? Sometimes they
had reasons for the thing, like eating people or stealing
water, sometimes they didn't. Maybe the aliens were
environmentalists, and they saw what we were doing to our

                                                      7

planet, and it was like when I weed a garden so that some
will grow higher. I'm telling you, I think they wanted to fix
us.

SIMS

We're in a a big SIMS game. Like that movie, the Matrix -
you never watched the Matrix, how have you never watched
the Matrix? It sucks that you can't ever now ever. The
sequels sucked, so you didn't miss much, except the KEY
TO THE UNIVERSE. Come on, it makes sense. IT MAKES
SENSE! We're like minds inside a computer simulation.
Have you thought about it, like, how does any one of us
know if the others exist, right here, right now? Like, so
maybe I'm the only one who exists - or just you and me? We
couldn't know, you know. Our whole experience happens in
our brains, you know. It could be like a billion years in the
future and we're in these pods with tubes stuck to us, and
there was a glitch, bzst, and the system was overloaded and
it deleted the files of everyone over the - that's why the age
is so specific, you know. Or, like in the Matrix, they harvest
people of a certain age and —

POLITICAL

Government. You remember when the dude wanted to fire
nuclear missiles at hurricanes? At hurricanes! Well, he sure
got his wish. I bet you there was some red button on his
desk, which he confused for, I don't know- and maybe it
wasn't a mistake, it was intentional - people like that, they
assume reality is going to shape itself to what they say, and
they commit to that reality, THAT WAS THE NATURE OF
BEING AN ADULT, they'd blow up the world before
admitting being wrong. It was like OLD DUDE

PSYCHOLOGY. At least we don't wake up to whatever
political trash is going on every day.

RELIGIOUS
It has to be God. Or a God. Who else but God could make
such a large scale miracle? Miracles don't have to be good.
Old Testament God smote all but a handful of the animals
and like Moses. Why don't you think He wouldn't do it
again? To wipe humanity of all the wickedness? And then
there's *The Rapture*. Maybe they missed something when
they wrote the Bible, like they lost a page with the part
where the young and innocent are left behind. Or, like a
different God, like Loki, read the Bible, was inspired, and so
this is like the HEB store brand version of the rapture?

SCIENTIFIC
It's obviously some scientific experiment. When they did the
first nuke test, they didn't know everything - could have set
the world on fire. Same with the Large Hadron Collider. So
that's what it was. They turned on some machine, and it
opens some time portal. They did stuff like that all the time,
all the time. CFC's blowing holes in the ozone. Styrofoam,
let's make something that lasts forever. That stuff that was in
baby bottles. That non-stick stuff. Cell phone brain cancer
radiation. Fracking. I guarantee, *guarantee*, Jeff Bezos had
some weird crap going on, or Google, Google had enough
power, they could have just been like, let's do this
experiment. There's no profit in a dead world, but there was
always a profit in killing it.

CONSPIRACY
What if the second wave wasn't connected to the first? What
if that one was kids - young kids, you know, Firestarters?

CONSPIRACY (CONT)

You don't know that, there could be lots of fire starters we don't know about. A bunch of them, so many of them got together to 'cleanse' the world.

HIDING (probably a very young person)

They are all hiding.
I think they're playing a game. A big game. We'll find them. We got to find them, we just gotta get past the bad stuff.

ENVIRONMENTAL

The planet just couldn't sustain us all. It coughed us up. It's a matter of evolution.

MAGIC

A magician! A witch! A genie! A curse.
Some first-grader made a wish on a monkey's paw, and we're like this until she learns a lesson.

The timer ends.

SCRAPPER

30 more seconds.

BOLT

No.

SHANE

OMG. Who the hell cares?!

BOLT	SCRAPPER
Language.	I care! 30 —

SHANE

It's a waste of time.

SCRAPPER

Not if we figure it out.

BOLT

That's not the point of Argument Circle.

SCRAPPER

Why aren't we out there LOOKING for them, you cowards!

SHANE

Because they're dead. All that matters is the mess they left behind.

SCRAPPER

Firestarter!

BOLT

HEY HEY HEY - do we need to separate you two? One minute is one minute.

ALL

One minute is one minute.

SCRAPPER

And we don't say 'dead.'

BOLT

That, too. Shane, we don't say "d—."
Matter doesn't disappear.

ALL

Matter doesn't disappear.

BOLT

Now. Everyone make up. We're making a world here, guys.
Let's make it beautiful and kind.

> *The Altierra crew begrudgingly makes up with*
> *one another.*

T

One minute. Once a week. So we don't obsess. Get it out.
Don't look at the sun, don't think too much. Keep moving.

BOLT

Alright, Altierra. Next on the agenda — Food?

> *Everyone picks a subject that they want to speak*
> *about. The conversation becomes teenage chaos,*
> *and it's frustrating to BOLT as it goes on too*
> *long and nothing is really decided.*
> *It can be largely improvised.*
> *One thing of note: MATH is in charge of water,*
> *and there's definitely a lack of it in March 2024,*
> *so this information may come out a little louder*
> *than the rest. An example of what some of the*
> *conversation could look like is below:*

EXAMPLE OF THE CONVERSATION

We should use the talking stick. I like the talking stick./
Everything in the outdoor garden looks sick. We really could
use some more *water,* for it -
MATH: Pray for rain. /
Can we use some on the vegetables?
MATH: If you want to haul it from Barton Springs, be my
guest.
Can you do that without the attitude? We're just asking for a
little water so we have something fresh.

MATH: I didn't cause global warming, moron.

Hey! Don't be a jerk.

You should get water from the springs.

Rock-Paper-Scissors for it.

Kayla and Michael are loving biology. We'll totally get a new medic once Adam is raptured.

Dude. What are you doing talking about me like I'm not here?

T

This is pretty typical.

BOLT
(overlapping with the chaos)
Is everyone done?

LOR coughs. SCRAPPER notices.

SCRAPPER
I got one thing, I got one thing, I got one thing.
(yelling over everyone)
Mr. Avers is a month late.

(Uh oh. A beat, then:)

DJ
Anyone want to talk about what we think happened to Mr. Avers, yo?

SHANE   MATH
I do.   My money's on gators.
                                   Florida, you know.

DJ
I bet he met someone. Fell in love.

13

OZLI

Fairies!

ALTIERRA'S SIMULTANEOUS SPECULATION
(more improvised chaos)

Acid rain melted him.

He got lost.

I heard there are like zombie wolves. Zombie wolves got him.

He's radioactive.

He fell off his bike. He's injured in a ditch, all broken apart and bloody.

He found a better place, and he sold us out. I heard there's a city called Eden with thousands of people.

He got robbed. He's so full of shame. So sad.

The Firestarters got him.

Maybe he got old and the rules changed again.

BOLT

Okay, okay, HEY! This is not useful. Are we done? Is everyone complete?

SHANE

What will we do if he doesn't get here?

SCRAPPER

We should find him.

ADAM

That's not safe.

SCRAPPER

WE SHOULD FIND HIM. WE SHOULD DO SOMETHING! SOMETHING!

BOLT

He'll get here.

SCRAPPER

He has supplies!
Let's put it to a vote. Raise your hand to send a search party!

*(only SCRAPPER raises his hand. He grabs
whoever is closest.)*

SCRAPPER

Raise your hand, raise it -

SHANE

You want to lose that hand?

MATH

East is danger.

BOLT

Mr. Avers was a Scout and he's like almost twenty. He'll be
fine, okay? He's fine.
Anything else?

A collective shrug.

SCRAPPER

But—

BOLT

Meeting adjourned.

They begin to leave. T is back to interviewing.

T

Adam, what did you do on Day Zero?

ADAM

Cried a lot. Why are you asking this?

T

It's for the Apocalypse Project.
What about you?

DJ

Weapons. Was super into Ren Faires back then, so…
weapons made sense.

T

You?

SHANE

Dude. It doesn't matter. Your video doesn't matter. Momma
nature's wiping us off and starting fresh. And one of the best
things about the apocalypse is that the internet is dead.

They leave. T is alone.

T

Someday, the internet could come back to life, and there will
be a chronicle of all this.
Youtubers were like the scribes of internet times.
It's a time capsule? A vlog. Or a poem.
So, in case this is far in the future, and some other animal
has evolved to replace us fleshy, fragile apes, and they - you
— are trying to piece together what happened to this planet
—
This is my life, here at Altierra. Greenhouse, water, crying
room —

T (CONT)

I grew up around here.
It's sad.

TWO- Mr. Avers Returns
The Apocalypse Project - April 2024

One of the kids is leading an 'Altierra Video Game'[2].
The AVG is something like Fortnite, the video game?, only instead of this being an actual video game, they do it in the style of a tabletop storytelling game.
T unplugs the phone from the hutch and powers it on. Someone is right there next in line to plug something she really wanted to use, like a rechargeable fan.

T
Hey future fan-squad. I got power! This is T coming at you with the Apocalypse Project. April 2024.
        (T's music hum drum)
I managed to save enough energy for another update.

BOLT
Lights out, my dudes.

The crew gathers blankets for the night.

OZ
Who plays "Mom" tonight?

LOR
I think it's Adam's turn to be Mom.

SCRAPPER
No. He's lousy at being Mom.

---

[2] Yet another thing that can be replaced with whatever is popular at the time of production.

                    OZ

Adam's a bad mom.

                    DJ

I miss bacon.

                    LOR

Adam is Mom tonight.

                    OZ

Remember Sarah? Sarah was awesome at being Mom. She
sounded just like a mom.

          ADAM appears. He's in 'mom' drag.
          If this actor is a guy, perhaps this could seem to
          be a 'boy in a dress' joke, but then ADAM begins
          to read, and any levity softens into grief.
          The book is Peter Pan.

"All children, except one, grow up. They soon know that
they will grow up, and the way Wendy knew was this."

          This can go on for a little while. Use the actual
          text from Peter Pan.
          As he reads, we see the kids react.
          It's painful, and LOR is hurt the most.

                    LOR

Uh. I need to go.

          LOR leaves.

                    SHANE

Wimp.

*We hear the sound of tin cans. A sort of
rudimentary alarm system.
The kids immediately spring into action. This
could be an emergency, and they'd trained for
this.
They're scrambling, and fear is obvious, but
they've also done this many times.*

OZ

What's that? WHAT'S THAT??

BOLT
(voice)

Math, check it from the topside. I'm on suit. DJ, get the
geiger. Adam, emergency lights.

MATH checks it out.

OZ

I bet it's a firestarter!

ADAM

Oz — Shhhhhut up

MATH returns.

ADAM

Mr. Avers?

MATH

Probably.
Y'all, get something pointy just in case.

*BOLT enters in what looks like a radiation suit
and a Geiger counter from DJ.*

SHANE, DJ, LOR, and others have pointy things.
Everyone is on edge for what could be approaching.
A figure enters.
His head is covered by a mask.
And he's singing. The song is muffled.

MATH

Lights!

ADAM turns on the emergency lights.
A beat.
BOLT approaches the figure, then uses the radiation detector.
It clicks a bit, but not too much.
BOLT does a thumbs up.
Then there's a secret greeting between BOLT and Mr. AVERS - a handshake that means you are part of Altierra.

BOLT

Welcome back, Mr. Avers.

Mr. AVERs takes off his mask.
THE ALTIERRA CREW greets him with cheers, their fear instantly turned to joy.
Their eagerness overwhelms him.

Mr. AVERS

Settle down, settle down. Mr. Avers has things to say.

T
(to the camera)

Mr. Avers is bringing us some important, imported contraband.

Mr. AVERS

I BROUGHT SO MUCH CANDY! SETTLE DOWN IF
YOU WANT IT!
Call me, Santa, I come bearing gifts. Direct from Capetown,
South Africa

T

Where there's people still making things.

Mr. AVERS

They've traveled so far. The gifts, not me. I crossed no ocean
- I crossed something far more dangerous - America - or
what's left of the old gal.

OZ

Santa?

Mr. AVERS

Actually don't call me that. Santa had it easy. Santa didn't
have to deal with radiated dogs and pirates and flat tires and
broken spokes. T, is T still alive?

T

Here.

Mr. AVERS

Oh, good. I figured that if they turned anyone into kibble it
would be you. Glad we haven't hit level cannibalism yet. T,
why are you so slow? Find a pen. We got maps to update!
Now, T - cross out Miami. It's done. Underwater, and worse,
some kids figured out how to do war-ships, so now we got
honest to dog pirates up and down the coast.

T

Miami is… gone. I never went to Miami.

(This hits SHANE hard.)

SHANE

It was a good city.

Mr. AVERS

Overrated. Now, Tallahassee, that was gem! Cross
Tallahassee out, too.

T

No Tallahassee??

Mr. AVERS

I heard Pittsburgh is on it's way out. All those bridges. So
much rust.

T

I wanted to see Pittsburgh.

Mr. AVERS

I got more where that comes from - because along with fifty
boxes of Red Vines, 427 Snickers, 500 protein bars, and six
crates of Very Important Medications and PPE, I bring
stories, STORIES, and map edits. Here - take this.
(Mr. AVERs tosses T a notebook with notes)
It's the latest version, full of geographical gossip. America,
2.0—
Now. Lugging hundreds of pounds behind him, Mr. A
pedaled thousands of miles dodging chemical and nuclear
fallout and ALLIGATORS, and no one has ever been so
saddle sore - so I beg you to please unload the cart for poor
Mr. Avers. Oh, and someone get me something to drink.

SCRAPPER

I'll get it.

> *SCRAPPER is about to head out, but then he hears:*

Mr. AVERS

Lor!

> *(SCRAPPER turns to hear what Mr. AVERS says to LOR)*

Everyone else calls me Mr. Avers, but you, I wants you to call me "my hero," or possibly, 'Your highness," or maybe, "My God!" And I'll call you old wheezy.

> *Mr. AVERS tosses LOR an asthma inhaler.*

LOR

Thank you. This should last the rest of my life.

THREE - Exile

They exit.
Then we are with SCRAPPER -
Who is getting water.
And is deeply upset.

SCRAPPER

This thing won't work. WHY IS IT SO SLOW??

….

Lor, why do you SAY things like that?

Why does he say things like that? "The rest of his life." He doesn't know, he doesn't. Anything can happen. They could come back. We could find them.

> *SHANE is there. SHANE is devastated at the*
> *news about Miami, but hiding it, and SHANE is*
> *the type to cover pain with anger.*

SCRAPPER

Go away, Shane.

SHANE

Shane in the shiny jacket disturbs the scrap, still upset.

SCRAPPER
(overlapping)

All you got is that jacket, but no heart under it. And so no one cares what you have to say.

Oh, who's that talking? No one cares who is talking? Stop talking. STOP TALKING! STOP TALKING!

SHANE

*(As SHANE says this, SCRAPPER gets more and
more upset and in SHANE's face)*

They did the ADULT thing. They ABANDONED US. But
know what? It was the only GOOD thing they did in their
lives. I'm glad they're dead. Your brother's gonna be gone.
Like Houston. Like Galveston. Like Miami. Like your
favorite teacher, like every member of Congress and Taylor
Swift and Lizzo and Bill Nye and your racist uncle and your
doctor and your Grandma and your mom! And my mom!
AND SOON YOUR BROTHER AND ME AND YOU! And
WE ARE ALL BETTER FOR IT!

SCRAPPER

I WISH YOU WOULD DISAPPEAR! EVERYONE
WISHES YOU WOULD DISAPPEAR!

*SCRAPPER punches SHANE in the face.
SHANE hits back.
They fight.
Their scuffle knocks over the power box.
The lights flicker.
The fight breaks the water storage container.
Water flows out.
LOR and T race in, followed by OZ.*

OZ

They're fighting! They're fighting!

LOR	T
Hey, stop that, stop that,	The water!
Scrap —	

LOR pries SCRAPPER from SHANE.

SCRAPPER
WHY ARE YOU TAKING HIS SIDE?

> *SCRAPPER breaks away, kicking SHANE, and
> hitting OZ, who begins to cry, and knocking T to
> the ground.*
> *BOLT enters.*

BOLT
WHAT'S GOING ON HERE!

> *BOLT rings the bell.*
> *EVERYONE else enters.*
> *The fight is broken up.*

SHANE
That one attacked me.

SCRAPPER
You deserved it!

> *MATH turns off the water.*
> *ADAM tends to OZ's bloody nose.*

MATH
What is wrong with you?? You broke our water, you selfish
thoughtless—

BOLT
Look, LOOK! I'm not angry, just disappointed.

SHANE
YOU ARE NOT THE BOSS!

                    OZ
Yeah she is.

                  SHANE
Scrapper started it.

                   BOLT
He's just a kid

                  SHANE
We all are.
Every single one of us on the effing planet is a kid.

                   BOLT
LANGUAGE!
You two have been itching for this for a while.
Math. What's the damage?

                   MATH
Well, the water's broken.

                  ADAM
Duh.

                   BOLT
Can we fix it?

                   MATH
Yeah, but...
Still be close to empty.
Til there's rain.

          A panic grips the Altierra kids, and they all start
          talking at once.

BOLT

Everyone! Group breath.
In
two three.
Out
two three.
Panic helps no one.
Okay. We're low on water. That's a problem. Every
problem's got a solution.
We can dig a well.

MATH

We had one. Deep. It's dry.

BOLT

We can fill up canteens at Barton Springs. Use grey water on
the vegetables.

SHANE

Mmmm Mmm e-coli salad.

MATH

WE ALREADY DO THAT!

They all erupt.

ADAM

Will you shut up I got the talking stick

DJ

Are we doing the talking stick thing? I thought we stopped
doing that?

ADAM

I think we should because people are not shutting up!

MATH

Then I take it -
(MATH snatches the talking stick)
Do we gotta spend all day going back and forth pretending
we can't see what's in front of our eyeballs? We're dry. We
got more thirsty mouths than we got water to fill em.

LOR

What's it going to matter? In two years, you'll have plenty of
bedspace.

ADAM
(taking the stick)
Point being, we can't keep the place going. There will be
more fights.

BOLT

But we can do it. Hikes to the spring. Conflict mediation.

MATH
(taking the stick back)
We're already doing that, and we're still scraping bottom.
Hiking takes calories - and calories take water.
The math doesn't work.

BOLT

We'll figure it out.

MATH

We gotta lose some people.

BOLT

End of discussion

ADAM

It's not your decision, B.

MATH

Sarah made Altierra a pure democracy. You ain't in charge.

LOR

Her word matters.

MATH

Fine.
Then listen to me, Bolt, and the rest of you, too.
You hippie Bolton sisters got future in your brains, so put this thought into it. I do this math every day, and I figure we gotta shed about four people right now.
Else… we take the compound apart and spread out.

T

We could do that.

ADAM

Move closer to the river. Put up tents.

MATH

And no more Altierra.

This hits BOLT.

BOLT

Four people?

MATH

Four.

BOLT

…On Day Zero, when oil wells were blowing and planes fell out of the sky, and everyone was screaming for mom and dad, my sister Sarah, she kept her brain. She knocked down doors looking for babies. And she found them, she found you. And she made this place for them, for us, a home - a place of peace.
A place to make a future.
This is for her. For Sarah. Wherever she is.
Four people?

The group nods in agreement.

BOLT

How? We draw lots?

MATH

No! We keep the most useful, cut the fat.

BOLT

NO ONE IS "FAT!"

ADAM

I think it should be a popularity contest!

Mr. AVERS

Well, I'm kinda used to being out on the road myself. So, I volunteer.

MATH

Oh, I assumed you wouldn't stay. So, five need to go counting Mr. Avers.

BOLT

Here's the hard truth: We can't have people starting fights here. We got small ones.

MATH

And he broke the water.

A murmur. No one fights this.

SHANE

I know when I'm not wanted.

SCRAPPER

Oh now you do?

BOLT

I meant Scrapper.

SCRAPPER

What??

LOR

Shane should go.

SHANE

Dude.

BOLT

It takes two to fight.

LOR

He's a kid.

BOLT

As Shiny Jacket established - we all are. You both need to
go.

SHANE

Good.

GOOD!

I'm done with you.

BOLT

Shane.

SHANE

What? No one here likes me enough to protest.

SHANE leaves.

MATH

That's two. Now, Scrap —

LOR

I should go in his place. Send me away. He's young -

BOLT

And he starts fights.

SCRAPPER

I should go, Lor.

MATH

Three.

LOR

Then I'm going, too.

SCRAPPER

You're sick. You're like a weak antelope sick. You're like
lazy fungus sick. You're like -

LOR

I got about two years left in my hourglass, and there are
some small ones with a lot more left, so let me do this for
you - for the greater good. I got my inhaler. I got good legs. I
can make it far enough —

SCRAPPER

Make him stay! Make him stay.

LOR

It's my choice.

BOLT

It's his choice.

LOR

I made it.

MATH

That's four. One more.

SCRAPPER

This is so bad.

LOR

You're getting your wish, Scrapper. We can see things — the
Grand Canyon! Yosemite! Or find another place, somewhere
safe - New Eden -

SCRAPPER

New Eden doesn't exist.

LOR

We'll find another place —
We can even go back, you know, home —

SHANE
(poking their head back in)
Maybe your Mom will be waiting for you.

SCRAPPER

Can I punch him one more time?

BOLT

Anyone else?

OZ

I think Math should go. He's ugly.

MATH

Will you shut up?

The others argue amongst themselves.

ADAM

I SAY WE TAKE A VOTE! I GOT OPINIONS! On the
count of three, we all say who should leave.

BOLT

What, wait, no.

ADAM

One, two —

                                    T

No need!
Friends! I nominate myself. I was born a mile away, I have
ALWAYS been safe - cared for by you, and you, and you.
But I want danger. I want - the world. I want to bear witness
to what's happening to this country, this generation, and
make it immortal. You know, through youtube-videos.

                                  BOLT

And that's number five.
Just because you can't stay doesn't mean we don't love you.
In a few years, you'll come back. The water will be back.
The garden will be beautiful.

                                  LOR

I don't got a couple years.

                                SCRAPPER

YEAH YOU DO!

                                  BOLT

DJ will get your bikes set up with trailers and packs and the
lights that charge when you pedal.

                                   DJ

Wait, really? Why do I gotta —

                                  BOLT

You'll have food, water filters, tents, equipment — and a
copy of the library.

                                    T

Yes!

BOLT
You'll also have - our love, respect, and appreciation. Cool?

LOR
Cool.

BOLT
Cool.

OTHERS
Cool.

LOR
Mr. Avers. We would like to go west. Can you plot a course for us?

Mr. AVERS
No doy, travel-bugs, no doy.

FOUR- Bad Omen.
On the Road
It's a month later.
The four of them are riding bikes.
T takes out her phone and films. Which is not
exactly safe.

T

So. The Apocalypse Project. May 2024.
(T chirps an intro song)
And, uh, Texas! — has a lot of… space. And bugs. I've
been trying to figure out what poetic things to say about the
space, but nothing comes.
It's space.

Mr. AVER is singing.

Mr. AVERS
(singing)
I like to ride my bicycle
I like to ride my bike
I like to ride my bicycle
You say left, I say right.
I want to ride my BICYCLE!

SCRAPPER
Those aren't the lyrics.

Mr. AVERS
How would you know? Did you Google it? No, you didn't
because Google is dead.

T

The roads are mottled, broken with grass, weeds, heavy with silt and sand. We ride by abandoned towns lousy with sagging houses.

LOR

Don't fall. You're making me worried.

SCRAPPER

Let her fall. We might get lucky and it will break her mouth off.

> *T sticks her tongue out and goes back to filming - and riding one handed.*

T

I used to think buildings kept people safe and whole.
Now I know that a house without a someone inside falls apart, like it needs a human to hold the rafters up.

Mr. AVERS

Welcome to New Mexico, folks.

T

We find a lot of dead cars. Tires flat, keys in the ignition, half-buried in sand. They will never get where they were going. Sometimes we sleep in them— bugs — but there's nothing like the night skies.
Light pollution burned away, so many star—
And I'm out of power.
Hey! BAD NEWS, guys. My generator's broken. This is gonna set the Apocalypse Project back, you guys.

SCRAPPER

Yeah. Bad. News.

                           LOR

Well, you didn't need to document our descent into madness.
Though it would probably make good content.

                            T

You're jealous that my phone works and yours doesn't.

                           LOR

I'm really not.

                         SCRAPPER

Youtuber drama.

                        Mr. AVERS

I'm a killer Queen
Shot a guy with a lazerbeam
Bah bah—

                    They slow and stop.
                    A beat.
                    Mr. AVERS points, suddenly serious.

                            T

Buzzards.

                           LOR

Could be animal.

                         SCRAPPER

Could be a Firestarter.

                           LOR

Probably an animal.

                                                          41

Mr. AVERS

Lorenzo. Get something with a point.

> *LOR grabs a weapon. He and Mr. AVERs go*
> *ahead.*
> *A beat. T and SCRAPPER are nervous.*

T

Vultures are important members of the ecosystem.

SCRAPPER

Symbolic, too.

> *Thunder.*

SCRAPPER

Storm coming. Should find shelter.

T

We passed a U-Haul a mile or so back.

SCRAPPER

There was a family of raccoons in it.

T

Raccoons are cute

SCRAPPER

And tasty.

> *LOR and Mr. AVERS return. LOR is ashen.*

LOR

It's a deer.

                    SCRAPPER

Are you —

                      LOR
                (it wasn't a deer)
A deer. Let's get going.

                       T
Are you going to sing, Mr. Avers?

                      LOR

No he's not.

                   Mr. AVERS

I think no.

            They ride.

            Something has darkened.

            Thunder thunder.

                      LOR

Mr. Avers! Storm.

                       T
We passed a U-Haul about a mile ago.

                    SCRAPPER

We can turn around —

                      LOR
WE'RE NOT GOING BACK!
We're not, okay?

T

It's starting to sprinkle.

It rains.

FIVE - St. Mikey's Academy and Fortress

*Inside the fortress, BRAT and the BOOT stalk
the door and look at security footage.
They are dressed in well-pressed school
uniforms that hit more militaristic notes.
We can hear the rain outside.*

BOOTLICKER

I say we just stab 'em. Brat, Brat! Did you hear me? I made
a suggestion, Brat.

BRAT

I got ears. It'll make a mess. Go get the Headmaster.

BOOT

He's watching stories.

BRAT

Go get him anyway. This could be a Trojan situation, like we
learned.

BOOT

I outrank you, Brat.

BRAT

No you don't.

BOOT

I do. I'm a tenth-grader. You're in ninth. You're practically
junior high, Brat.

BRAT

My scores are higher than yours, Bootlicker.

Knock knock knock.

Mr. AVERS (voice)

Hello!
Excuse me! I am William Clinton Avers of Austin, Texas, my pronouns are he/him. I come in peace.

The others start to introduce themselves.

BOOT

They come in peace. That's gotta be a trick.

BRAT

Summon the Headmaster. This is a Trojan situation.

Mr. AVERS

We are but weary travelers seeking shelter in your windmill-powered bunker. It's real bad out here. Like a six, maybe seven.

T

And I'd like to plug in my phone. If that's cool.

BRAT

You gotta negotiate with our Headmaster.

The HEADMASTER appears with BOOTLICK following behind.

HEADMASTER

This better be an emergency! I was watching my favorite episode of *Friends*.

BOOT

It may be a Trojan situation.

HEADMASTER
Who interrupts the exploits of Ross and Chandler? Speak now, unless the wolves have taken your lips.

Mr. AVERS
I am William Clinton Avers, my pronouns are —

HEADMASTER
I really don't care, hippie.

LOR
It's raining, we need shelter.

Mr. AVERS
We're travelers from the great state of Texas!

SCRAPPER
Have you heard of it?

LOR
They're not morons, they've heard of Texas.

Mr. AVERS
How about a trade?

HEADMASTER
… You may enter if you agree to Our Rules. Rule Number One, I make the rules.

BRAT
We got harpoons aimed at you.

BOOT
They call us "silent but deadly."

HEADMASTER
That is not the name. We do not call them that.

The door is opened.

HEADMASTER
What do you have to trade?

Mr AVERS
We got Red Vines, and they're still good.

BOOTLICKER
Oooh.

HEADMASTER
I do not permit sugar-as-currency in St. Mikey's.

Mr. AVERS
Oh, I was kidding then.

LOR
Four protein bars. One for each of us.

HEADMASTER
Those are full of sugar.

LOR
Drat.

Mr. AVERS
What else we got?

                              T
I got something

                          MR AVERS
Fake youtube videos.

                              T
Information. A map of the Great State of Texas and beyond.

                          HEADMASTER
No one in St. Mikey's ever leaves.

                              T
Um. How about a cornbread recipe?

                            BRAT
Oooh.

                          HEADMASTER
That's good for one of you. What else?

                              T
Instructions on composting.

                            BRAT
Hippies.

                              T
                  *(improvises something like: The schematics on a
                  diesel engine. / Instructions on fixing a printer.)*

                          HEADMASTER
Ah. Much better.

T
(offering from the Library binder)
Four pages now. You get the 5th when we leave.

HEADMASTER
Clever. Brat - get this to the photocopier.
(BRAT takes the pages.)
We like clever at St. Mikey's Academy and Fortress. Perhaps you'd like to join us—

SCRAPPER
Traveling is kinda our thing.

HEADMASTER
Did I say you could speak? No. This is your first infraction. Two more and you're expelled.
You are expected to behave as an adult while you are on the premises. Now, annoying one, please accompany Bootlicker - he'll show you where you can store your bikes.
(BOOT and SCRAPPER exit)
As for the rest of you: Welcome. The men's dormitory is to the right. The women's to your left. You're outsiders, so you will stay in the basement. If you pledge yourselves to me, you get a bed - after placement testing and we have inspected you thoroughly.
(Mr. AVERS is raising his hand.)
Yes, you may speak.

Mr. AVERS
We don't need beds. We're open-road type folks.

T
Yeah. We don't need separate dormies for rain.

HEADMASTER

There are many benefits to submitting yourself to me. I'm very good at authority.

LOR

You sure have a lot here.

HEADMASTER

Things get done when you have a strong leader. So long as the wind blows and our turbines move, we have every luxury of the beforetimes. We have working refrigerators, milk, an *ice machine*, laundry, air conditioning -

The crew moans. Oh man. AC.

HEADMASTER

Not to mention an extensive DVD collection, including every episode of *Baywatch*.

LOR

Oooh. I miss TV so hard.

HEADMASTER

I love Pamela Anderson[3]. If one could trade all of humanity minus her or have only her and no humanity, I'd pick Pamela in a heartbeat. I should have been born in the 80s.
On Thursdays, we have karaoke. It's mandatory.

LOR

This place is so… safe.

---

[3] You may substitute David Hasselhoff for Pamela Anderson.

HEADMASTER

We're very good at safety.
You have 'til morning, 8am sharp, to consider joining us.
(To LOR)
I can see by the glimmer in your eye, you're tempted. We've made a perfect society. Surely you'll agree.

Mr. AVERS

No. We're good.

HEADMASTER

To the basement then. You are not to leave the basement while with us. If you do, we have a graveyard out back where you can stay.

SIX - Things Go Boom

Then we're in the basement with T, SCRAPPER,
LOR, and Mr. AVERS.
T has plugged in her phone.

T

Hey T-niacs.
We're locked in the basement of a small authoritarian
windmill-powered — something.
Which sucks, but at least we're not wet - and we got
electricity.
        (bum bum bum)
And we got a DVD player.

> *LOR is watching a tiny DVD player and*
> *drinking a Diet Coke.*

LOR

Shhh. I'm watching *The Matrix*.

SCRAPPER

This suuuucks. We should have spent the night in a U-Haul
with raccoons.

LOR

We could still be in Altierra if you hadn't broken the water.

SCRAPPER

Shut up, Lor.

LOR

You shut up. Keanu is speaking.

SCRAPPER

You're not thinking of staying, are you?

LOR

Of course I am. And you should, too.

SCRAPPER, T, Mr. AVERS

What, no!

SCRAPPER

They'll make you wear those ugly uniforms. You'll look so tacky.

Mr. AVERS

And you'd have to be like them.

LOR

It's two years. I won't mind.

SCRAPPER

But -

LOR

I got meds, I know how to work, and if I got 21 months left, I might as well sleep in a bed and and eat warm food and wear clean clothing and not worry about becoming a meal for the vultures. And the rest of you should stay too. Here. They got *Full House*.

SCRAPPER

This place is perfect for you.

From the shadows, we hear:

COLLIN

Yo! You gotta help me out of here.

SCRAPPER

Who's there!?? Show yourself. I got pointy things.

COLLIN

Can you keep it down?

SCRAPPER

That doesn't answer my question!

Mr. AVERS

Dude, chill.

SCRAPPER

There is no chill in the apocalypse. Identify yourself!

COLLIN

I'm no one.

Mr. AVERS

Okay, we're not dumb.

SCRAPPER

Lor is.

We see more of COLLIN.

COLLIN

Call me CB then.

Mr. AVERS

Are you a Firestarter, CB?

COLLIN

Nah I'm not. Can't stand 'em. I need your help.

Mr. AVERS

With what?

COLLIN

To get out.

LOR

Did you do something?

COLLIN freezes a bit. He's listening.

COLLIN

The storm is fssh fsshhh.
I gotta get out. Please.

LOR

Maybe we should call a guard — Boot—

COLLIN

Don't!

Mr. AVERS

Who are you?

COLLIN

Someone who flunked inspection. Someone who needs to
leave.

COLLIN freezes.

COLLIN

No more rain.

LOR

Why does that matter?

COLLIN

Can't bury someone when it's raining.

A noise - a door unlocking.
BRAT and BOOT enter.

LOR

Hey. You guys have the *Matrix* sequels?

BRAT points to Mr. AVERS.

BRAT

You're the leader.

T

We're more of a collective—

Mr. AVERS

I'm the leader.

BOOT

Come with us. NOW

Mr. AVERS

What, no! I don't consent to this AH—

They yank him offstage.
Slam. Lock.

T

Fam-squad! They just yeeted him —

COLLIN

Oh oh oh oh oh.

T

What's happening?

COLLIN

He told the Headmaster, 'no,' didn't he?

LOR

Mr. Avers follows his own bliss.

> *We hear yelling.*
> *A shot.*

SCRAPPER

What was that what was that?

COLLIN

No one leaves St. Mikey's.

T

I liked Mr. Avers so much.

> *A moment.*
> *The threat sinks in and SCRAPPER, T, LOR*
> *panic.*

LOR

This is a dream. Pinch yourselves. Wake up. Wake up.

SCRAPPER

Still want to stay, Lor?

I'm going to be sick.
He's fine, I'm sure he's —

COLLIN

That's not — no, man, no.

An alarm goes off.

COLLIN

That's new.

LOR

What's that?

COLLIN

An alarm.

LOR

What's it mean?

COLLIN

I don't know.

BRAT
(voice)
FIRESTARTERS! FIRESTARTERS!

COLLIN

Firestarters apparently.

HEADMASTER
(voice)
ST. MIKEY'S! THIS IS NOT A DRILL LIKE LAST
WEEK! THIS IS REAL!
BOOT, grab me a hostage -

BOOT enters the basement.

BOOT
TROJANS! You brought them here, didn't you!?

LOR
WHAT'S GOING ON???

BOOT
We're under attack, duh. You!

T
Me.

BOOT
You're a hostage.

BOOT tries to grab T as the others protest.
BOOT hits LOR with a club.

LOR
You hit me.

BOOT
I outrank you, so I hit you.

HEADMASTER

(voice)

GET TO THE RIGHT SIDE! YOUR OTHER RIGHT!
WHAT'S THAT SMOKE! WHERE'S THE HOSTAGE!

BOOT

Come with me

T

No!

COLLIN

Let her go! I AM AN ADULT AND YOU DO WHAT I SAY
KID.

> *BOOT is leveling a weapon at COLLIN when a*
> *FIRESTARTER enters and knocks BOOT away.*
> *Then, there's crazy chaos. We hear the sounds*
> *of yelling - a great fight is going on, alarms -*
> *offstage.*
> *Fire and smoke.*
>
> *The FIRESTARTER wins the grappling fight*
> *with BOOT.*
>
> *The FIRESTARTER looks at the crew. Then*
> *turns and leaves.*
> *The crew realizes that they can escape.*
> *They leave.*

SEVEN - Collin Beck

On the road. Again. No bikes, but there are
backpacks.
The crew is exhausted and upset.
Well, except COLLIN, who is excited to be free.

T

It's morning.
We can still smell the smoke. It's in our clothes.
We grabbed what we could and fled on foot.
I have two percent battery left. And with that two percent I
will say: I liked Mr. Avers. I will miss him.
       (a moment of silence)
… That's what I would say if my PHONE WASN'T DEAD!
My phone's dead.

SCRAPPER

Good.

T

Dude.

SCRAPPER

It matches Mr. Avers.

T

That wasn't my fault. Lor wanted to stay on the murder farm.

LOR

Shut up.

SCRAPPER

Yeah. Because they had TV. What a weak-willed bro-ski,
tempted by TV.

COLLIN BECK

I love this so much! The open road.

> *The ALTIERRA crew look at COLLIN, whose
> mood is far different from theirs.*

LOR

You're not mourning.
> *(LOR gives T and SCRAPPER a look that
> means, we need to figure this thing out, we can
> fight later.)*

Hey, so.
How about we talk about who you are? "CB."

COLLIN

I'm no one.

> *SCRAPPER and T respond by putting CB to the
> ground.*

LOR

I don't trust NO ONE anymore.
Search him.

> *They search him. They find an ID and hand it to
> LOR.*

COLLIN

I found that. I swear.

SCRAPPER

It's your picture. Collin Beck. CB.

LOR

Collin Beck is an organ donor. Moral choice.

COLLIN

Don't take my organs please.

LOR

Look at this.

T

No way.

SCRAPPER

That's so fake.

LOR

This says you're 23.
No one is 23.
Explain.

COLLIN

Fine. FINE.
Hi. I'm Collin Beck.
I'm 23, and I've always looked young for my age. I came
into this world three months before I was supposed to, and
maybe that's why they threw me back.

LOR

Who?

SCRAPPER

Yeah! Who??

COLLIN

You know who.

                    SCRAPPER

No we don't.

                       T

No one does.

                      LOR

Who?

                    COLLIN

The… others.

                      LOR

"Others."

                    SCRAPPER

Aliens?

                    COLLIN

Something like that. Yeah, no. Other beings. Could be from another planet, or dimension, or something else. Let's call them that. "Others."

                      LOR

We're nowhere near Roswell, if that's what's inspiring this b
—

                    COLLIN

Don't believe me. But I know. Okay. I know 'cause they took me along with the rest -
It was… Lights, sound, and the smell of - you don't want to smell that - like digestion.
And then they - like they said it, but they didn't say with words, they thought it, that's how they communicate, with like - thoughts? Or chemicals? Like — Zap brain -

COLLIN (CONT)
They said, I wasn't done yet. Zap brain.
Throw him back - like a fish. Zap brain.
And then I was in this slippery tube that was electric, and I
woke up in a field —
They took everyone in the world, rejected me.
And I don't care if you don't believe me.

SCRAPPER
And the others, the— not the. You know, the, our —

COLLIN
The oldsters? I think they're still alive. Like I'm 90%
certain.

LOR
Crazy.
Effing-crazy.
Well, Collin Beck, 23, it's been a pleasure knowing you, but
we gotta be on our way.

COLLIN
Don't leave me behind. Please don't. I can't…
I KNOW HOW TO FIND THEM.
Yeah.
The others communicate psychic-like, pew pew pew, and
they left this, this number in my brain. And I can't explain it
to you. It's like having a perfect banana bread recipe with a
thousand ingredients, only it's a recipe that will save
humanity. I'm NOT CRAZY. You gotta take me to the
White House.

LOR
The White House.

COLLIN

Yeah.

T

That's so gone.

COLLIN

No. Really? How do you know?

T
(about the library)
This map. Mr. Avers kept track of things.

COLLIN

Then... I need to go somewhere the internet works.

LOR

You need. The internet. For real.

SCRAPPER

How about the New Eden?

COLLIN

Sure, yeah. There. What's that?

LOR

It's a myth.

T

They say thousands live there. And it has working internet
and a functional government.

LOR

And rivers of peanut butter and jelly! Pocky grows from
trees and —

SCRAPPER

It's worth looking for.

COLLIN

We can get in touch with them, with this number in my brain
—

LOR

One sec — uh, talk amongst yourself.

T, LOR, & SCRAPPER huddle up.

T

What do we do?

LOR

I don't know.

SCRAPPER

Mr. Avers would know.

T

He would.

SCRAPPER

Lor. It seems impossible, but so does everything else we've ever known.

LOR

You believe him.

SCRAPPER

Yes. No. What else do we got?

LOR

… Yo. Collin Beck

COLLIN BECK

That's my name.

LOR

Right. Mr. Avers would say, the more the merrier. He would say it loud, and bragging about himself, but he would say it. And if he would, we will. Don't know where we're going. But you're free to join us along the way.

COLLIN picks up a backpack.

COLLIN

Well, then. We best get a move on.

As they leave, we hear SCRAPPER and LOR mutter and sing some Queen:

SCRAPPER

Is this the real life?

LOR

Or is this fantasy?

EIGHT - The Feral Child

LOR is looking at the map. The others are waiting.

LOR
No. No. Maybe… Okay.

T
Do you want me to — I'm the librarian.

LOR
I got it.
So… okay.

T
(narrating)
… So. Fam. We've been in California for about a week now
—

SCRAPPER
WHY ARE YOU VLOGGING WHEN YOUR PHONE IS
DEAD???

T
Practice.

*COLLIN is just the type to start conversations
with non sequiturs, and so —*

COLLIN BECK
Hey, have any of y'all ever been in love?

T
Nope.

SCRAPPY

With, like a person?

LOR

Never saw the need.

COLLIN

Scrapper, I've studied you, and you're the kind who stays single until later in life, and does stupid things along the way.

SCRAPPER

Cool.

COLLIN

That's the wisdom you get when you at 23. And because of me, you will get to be 23. T, you are the kind who thinks she's in love and gets engaged before graduating college and has a really messy breakup.

T

That's oddly specific.

COLLIN

Alien abduction power. CB's got WIZ-DUM. Lor, you are the kind of person—

LOR

This conversation ends now, Collin Beck.

SCRAPPER

Lor

                                 T
Have you ever been in love?

                              COLLIN
Yes. And maybe someday I'll even be loved back.

                                 T
You hear that?

                    Music? No. But, yes. Really? The sound is low,
                    scratchy or blistered.
                    They spot a tape player and outlet. There's a
                    note attached to it.

                              COLLIN
That, my dear, is a tape player.

                             SCRAPPER
What's a tape player?

                                LOR
You know what a tape player is.

                                 T
It's an outlet.
                    (about a note)
"I'll Give You the Sun." It's solar-powered, see.

                    (T is about to plug in her phone.)

                                LOR
What are you doing? That's not yours.

                                 T
It's for the Apocalypse Project.

COLLIN

This is like Bugs Bunny Wiley Coyote stuff.

SCRAPPER

Bugs Bunny?

COLLIN

Old person thing. Never mind.

LOR

You know what Bugs Bunny is.

SCRAPPER

What does Bugs Bunny have to do with a tape player?

COLLIN

It's a trap. Snap. That's what I meant.

T

It's not a trap. It's a gift.
It's meant for me.
        (A SHOCK)
Gah, it's bit me.

LOR

You —

>   *LOR goes to help -*
>   *An explosion.*
>   *Yeah, it was a trap.*
>   *The kids are thrown back —*

T

My phone.

A figure charges onstage, tackling LOR.
The figure is small. It's the child from the
prologue.

THE FERAL CHILD

Mine now! Mine! Mine!

The FERAL CHILD rips the library from LOR's
hand.

LOR

We need that!

FERAL CHILD

Mine mine mine!

The FERAL CHILD grabs at LOR's backpack.
The sound of a shot.
A FIRESTARTER appears.
The FERAL CHILD flees, taking the Library
with him.

SCRAPPER

That had the maps! We need that!

The FIRESTARTER fires into the air again.
Then reveals - a candybar.
This intrigues the FERAL CHILD, who returns.
The FIRESTARTER puts down the weapon.
The FIRESTARTER uses the candy to draw out
the FERAL CHILD.

FERAL CHILD

Candy?

The FIRESTARTER indicates - I'll trade you the candy for the library.

FERAL CHILD

It's mine. Mine!

The FIRESTARTER indicates: you want the candy? Give us the thing.

FERAL CHILD

CANDY! MINE NOW.

The FERAL CHILD grabs the candy but doesn't let go of the Library.
There's a tug of war, and the FIRESTARTER throws the FERAL CHILD to the ground.
The FIRESTARTER collects the weapon and levels it at the FERAL CHILD
There's a moment of intensity. Is the FIRESTARTER going to off the FERAL CHILD?

COLLIN BECK

No. Please! Listen to me, I am an adult - and he's just a kid - and please

FIRESTARTER lets the kid go. The FERAL CHILD flees, dropping the Library.
The FIRESTARTER reveals - the weapon is empty.

SCRAPPER

It's empty?

The FIRESTARTER picks up the abandoned Library.

LOR

We need it.

The FIRESTARTER hands the Library to LOR.

T

The feral child broke my phone.

SCRAPPER

YOUR PHONE ALMOST GOT US KILLED!

T

Preserving humanity is THE MOST IMPORTANT THING I
WILL EVER DO.

SHANE

No it's not.

*The FIRESTARTER takes off his mask and
reveals: It's SHANE.*

LOR

Shane!

SHANE

You're slow and easy to track.

COLLIN

You know him?

SCRAPPER

Unfortunately.

LOR

Should have recognized you by the jacket, huh?

T

I guessed it.

SCRAPPER

No you didn't.

LOR

How long you been following us, jerk?

SHANE

Hey. Raise your hand if you've saved Lor's ass?
Now raise the other hand if you did it a second time?
Interesting. Seems I shoulda earned some gratitude from
you.

LOR

I coulda taken him.

COLLIN

Me, too.

SCRAPPER

WHY have you been following us, Shane?

SHANE

Because you're soft and dumb and attract bullies like flies,
and I couldn't have you becoming worm-meat on my
conscience.
But if you don't need me, I can leave.
Do you want me to go? I'll go.
…You want me to go.   Fine. Everyone does.

T

Shane.
I want you to stay.

SHANE

No you don't.

LOR

If you want, stay.
I'd rather have you on our side.

COLLIN

You seem cool, edgelord.

SCRAPPER

And, I vote you stay, too.

SHANE
Ok.
Ok.
(then, to COLLIN)
Wait— who are you? And what did you mean, "I'm an adult."

NINE - End the Day

Around a fire.
They go to sleep.
A beat.
We see the FERAL CHILD.
The FERAL CHILD takes The LIBRARY and
shreds some pages before stealing it.

Act 2

ONE - Hindsight

A candle is lit or a flashlight is turned on.
It's something like a church service.
Everyone participates.

PASTOR

On this day, February 14, we honor the missing.
May they forever live on - like a brilliant meme burning
through our collective conscience.
They say hindsight is 20/20, the year when we last saw
them.
There's significance in that. Don't know what it is.
Now, let us bow and make hymns.
Join me:

> *THE PASTOR leads the crew in singing a hymn.*
> *This is is not a hymn you'd find in any holy*
> *book, but rather a hymn made up of lyrics from*
> *the songs immediately prior to the*
> *disappearance. Or, perhaps, it is a singular*
> *song, one that a member of the ensemble learned*
> *to love from their parents. We all have those*
> *songs, you know. I only know the Grateful Dead*
> *because my Dad put them on when his friends*
> *were over. Regardless, this is a moment that*
> *takes something you wouldn't think of as*
> *precious from the beforetimes and makes it*
> *graceful and communal.*
>
> *As it draws to a close, the lights are*
> *extinguished, the flashlights turned off.*

TWO - Mom and Dad Explain It All
March 2025

T turns on her phone.

                        T
What's up, descendants of pigeons, or cats, or cockroaches,

                  SCRAPPER
probably cockroaches

                        T
or whatever else has evolved to replace us homo-zapatos,
this is your buddy, T, coming at you from our campsite a bit
outside somewhere that used to be important in Oregon I
think.
It's March, 2025
                  (bum bum bee bum!)
And T gots herself a new phone -
                  (rah!)
Well not new-new, new-to-T-new.
A gift from your friend and mine —

                  SCRAPPER
A peace offering.

                        T
Admit it: you like me, too.

                  SCRAPPER
I'd be real sad if you fell off a cliff.

T

It's been a while since I could update. We've been traveling, and as we travel, we entertain people.

> *Lights up on COLLIN and LOR*
> *COLLIN has a big, very fake beard.*
> *LOR is in 'mom' drag.*
> *This is a performance for little kids.*

LOR

Hello little ones.

COLLIN

Howdy, howdy, youngsters.

LOR

My, how you've grown.

COLLIN

I got your nose.

LOR

Have you brushed your teeth?

COLLIN

Remember to make your bed!

LOR

Eat your veggies.

COLLIN

Be nice to you sister.

LOR

And feed the dog.

COLLIN
(indicating beard)
You can call me Poppa.

LOR
Call me Mama.

COLLIN
Once upon a time, grown-ups —

LOR
Big people.

COLLIN
Like us, only bigger and older.

LOR
With wrinkles.

COLLIN
And beards.

LOR
And grey hair.

COLLIN
If they had hair.

LOR
And no zits.

COLLIN
You may have seen pictures of them.

LOR
*(showing a presentation with old food packages
and stuff with pictures of adults)*

On signs and in old magazines and packages of Abuelitas hot chocolate.

COLLIN

These old people used to roam the lands —

*SHANE interrupts from a distance, like a
heckler.*

SHANE

Like dinosaurs.

LOR

Not like dinosaurs, no.

SHANE

Like locusts —/ No like monsters. Grrrrr -SNAP

COLLIN

Shane, we're getting like 10 candy bars for this.

SHANE

Telling them stories 'bout adults, right? Let's give them truth.

COLLIN

Are you drunk?

SHANE

I'm 21! I'm showing them another side of adulthood - drunk uncle side

LOR

Mama can deal with this.

COLLIN

I think this is a job for Papa Collin.
You. Come with me.

COLLIN exits, dragging SHANE with him.

T

Well, that part wasn't supposed to happen.
Sometimes I do Live Youtube! Challenges in the variety
show. I did the "Insect Eating Challenge"

SCRAPPER

Then you realized it's offensive.

T

Yeah. Some places eat bugs

SCRAPPER

It's good protein. And T shows up and is like, look how
gross I am, and we're in like, Minneapolis, and they're like,
yeah, it's Cricket-Taco Wednesday, have a cockroach
burger.

T

Look, I made an apology.
Anyway, in every town we visit, Scrapper and I go around
asking:

SCRAPPER to a TOWNIE

SCRAPPER

Yo, you know where I can find some internet?

T

Scrap is convinced that if we find a droplet of wi-fi, we can save the adults.

SCRAPPER

Collin is KEY. I'm a believer.

T

Me? I don't know.

SCRAPPER

He's the key!

T

… We don't have a good map anymore — we can only ask-hey, so where can we safely go next?
We're kind of adrift. South in winter, north in summer. We're migratory. Like Canadian geese!
Oh — there are so many birds now! Flocks that darken the skies for miles —
And, I've seen the Grand Canyon! Rocky Mountains! Joshua Trees! Yosemite! What used to be Phoenix!
As for our motley crew —
Um.
Let's make sure they're not about to kill each other.

> *Then we're with COLLIN and SHANE.*
> *SHANE is drinking.*

SHANE

Oh ho, gonna lecture me with your brain now? Zzzzap. I'm not going to apologize.

COLLIN

Like anyone can get through that shiny jacket—

SHANE

Your alien others took like FIVE BILLION OF YOU OLD
PEOPLE, and they rejected you. Huh.

COLLIN

Alright, firestarter drama queen, what's going on?

SHANE

You haven't wished me happy birthday, Alien Reject.
I am celebrating adulthood.

COLLIN

All this 'waa waa waa woe is I' is about aging?

SHANE

Nah. I love aging. I can do this finally. In a lawless land,
somehow we respect this one, like they're still watching over
us. Cheers. Granma Cruz always said, life would be better
with a two-martini high -

COLLIN

Shane.

SHANE

You're the one up there CELEBRATING THEM! There's
nothing wrong with me. Look in the MIRROR.

COLLIN

Look in the mirror your— .

SHANE

DON'T MYTHOLOGIZE THEM!

COLLIN

Why not?

SHANE

Collin Beck doesn't get it. Collin Beck can't. He's OLD.
Always looked young for his age, but he's an old person
with old person smell and old person soullessness.

COLLIN takes SHANE's flask.

COLLIN

Try me, birthday boy.

SHANE

Collin keeps trying to email aliens, to bring 'em back. And
he never stops to think, "What if I, just, don't."
Like what if this is supposed to happen?

COLLIN

Go on.

SHANE

You want to open this box? I don't think you do.

COLLIN

I do. Let the screaming demons fly screee. 100 percent.

SHANE

Yeah, right.

COLLIN

Go. On.

Big breath.

SHANE

Day Zero.

COLLIN

Day Zero.

SHANE

No one knew nothing. Alarms. Everyone confused, crying, screaming. The internet explodes - war?

COLLIN

Heh.

SHANE

Prank? Like some stupid movie - the adults all decided, let's teach kids how important old people are by disappearing - Know what I felt first?
Relief.
Don't gotta worry 'bout my old man. Or anyone's old man. Second, second, I felt panic.
You see, I was in Texas for a reason. My bleeding heart Tia Leti, brought me there to protest — pink hats, handwritten posters, all that — and she was gone — but her bloody heart was still there, and it pumps panic into me —
So, Day Zero, I stole, borrowed a truck, I had a learner's permit, and drove it THROUGH A HURRICANE to the border —
'cause that's where they had kids in cages.
Cages.
Tia Leti had told me about it, paid for me to be there so we could go yell at the guards, post things to your internet, like that woulda done anything more than make us feel good.
Some others got there first, but I saw 'em.

SHANE (CONT)

Covered in lice. Hungry. Eyes like hollow, like horror. Not because old people were gone, but because of what they'd done to them.

So screw you and Lor and everyone else painting a pretty picture of people who could —

I miss my Tia. And mom. And Granma Cruz in Miami. I do, but the one two third thing I felt?

Guess.

COLLIN

Guilt.

SHANE

…Yes.

COLLIN

Guilt because you get it, and you're supposed to be sad, but you're also thinking —

SHANE

I'm also thinking. Yeah. If I were God - and trying to fix the world - I'd start by getting rid of anyone over twenty myself.

COLLIN

Like you.

SHANE

Like me now. Cheers.

COLLIN

And like me.

SHANE

Yeah.
Like you.
Maybe.

COLLIN

I think there's something worth keeping.

SHANE

You're wrong.

COLLIN

Okay.

SHANE

You are.

COLLIN

Shane saved us - twice. Like Shane saved others, or tried to.
So maybe, maybe Shane thinks there's something in
humanity worth keeping.

SHANE

No.

COLLIN

So you wanna be a Firestarter? Burn it all down?

SHANE

… No.

COLLIN

If there's nothing worth saving.
Burn me down.
Go on.
I'm an adult. I can take it.
Set me on fire.
Make it all voosh.

SHANE

….
No.

COLLIN

Yeah I think there is something worth saving.

SHANE

…
Yeah?

COLLIN

Yeah.

SHANE

Yeah.
… um
I kinda want to kiss you right now.

COLLIN

How about when you're sober?

SHANE

That, too.

T

What?? What what?? Guys, that was so long coming!

                                COLLIN

Dude. T.

                                   T

And I got it on video.

                                COLLIN

Um. Let's finish this privately.

                                SHANE

Good, 'cause I gotta puke.

                                COLLIN

Romantic.

                                   T

I shipped them so hard, guys.

                    They exit
                    SCRAPPER returns, and he's a gusto of packing
                    up.

                                   T

Scrapper, I got some T on Shane and Collin. OMG I
SHOULD TOTALLY CALL THIS TEA WITH T!!

                               SCRAPPER

Spill it on the road.

                                   T

We just got here.

                               SCRAPPER

No internet. On to the next.

T

But.

SCRAPPER

WE DON'T HAVE FOREVER.

LOR enters with the TOWNIE, who is crying.

LOR

Let it out man. It's our job to make you cry. It's what we're good at.

TOWNIE

It's so sad - at the end of your book, the kid is holding his mom who is old. I want to hold my mom —
(hands LOR a candy bar)
A tip. For helping.

LOR

You gotta take care of the young or they will turn feral and explode you.

SCRAPPER

Lor! Pack up. This eight-grader who seemed stupid smart got me directions to another city, and promised me there's someone who knows where New Eden is. I traded him a shiny Pokemon card, so it darn well better be good.

TOWNIE

So beautiful, my man. You gotta come back.

LOR

Probably not. I'm turning 20 this summer.

SCRAPPER

No. WRONG. We'll be back. In one year's time, to the day,
I promise you. We all will. Go away now.

The TOWNIE exits.

T

I think she had a crush on you.

LOR

Nope nope! No time for romance. My life will be simple
from here on out.

SCRAPPER

Collin! Shane! We're going!

T

Um. They're busy.

THREE - A Trip to Sad Disneyland

T

A new city. We set up camp on the outskirts. Lor and Collin are rehearsing, Shane's brooding, and Scrap and I—

SCRAPPER

We got intel that there is connexiones out here. I can feel it - IN MY BONES.

T

I think you're starting to like the Apocalypse Project

SCRAPPER

Nope.

> *We hear…*
> *What is that? Is it an amusement park?*

(VOICE)

It's my turn to be the kid!

T

What's that sound?

SCRAPPER

Every time someone says, "What's that sound?" something awful happens.

A TEENAGER in CHILD DRAG enters.

TEENAGER in CHILD DRAG

FRIEND!

                    SCRAPPER
What, no, I have no friends.

                       T
You have me.

                    "CHILD"
You you, come with me. You're my best friend for the day.

                       T
What the —

                    SCRAPPER
Hell.

                    "CHILD"
Autograph! Excuse me, I'd like an autograph please.

                    A DISNEY-inspired costume character appears.
                    This costume is a bit worse for wear.
                    The CHILD gets an autograph from this
                    character,
                    The CHILD's autograph book is absolutely
                    covered in pen.

                    "CHILD"
Let's do a ride! You're my best friend, come on.

                    SCRAPPER
We're looking for the internet? Can you help us?

                    "CHILD"
You look sad. Best friends should not be sad.
You should have some fun.

CHILD hands SCRAPPER... is that DOLE WHIP?

"CHILD"

It's from the Ninchanted Tikli-Room!

SCRAPPER

The what?

DISNEY-CREATURES pop out with puppets that look like birds and flowers.
While dancing, they sing a verse of the song from the Enchanted Tiki-Room - or rather something like this song, like they tried to remember it but couldn't quite get it right.
It's weird and amazing, and distinctive enough no one would confuse it for the original IP.

T

They made a Sad Disneyland.

SCRAPPER

In the middle of nowhere.

The DISNEY-CREATURES sing another verse before whipping away.

T

It's nice there's no one to sue for copyright infringement.

SCRAPPER

Technically, I think it's a parody. There's Lor.
Oh God, no —

The DISNEY-CREATURES appear again as LOR finds SCRAP and T.

The DISNEY-CREATURES are acting robotic now.

Maybe they're carrying puppets. Maybe they are the puppets.

LOR

Scrap, what the hell is this?
This is so weird.

T

I think it's fun.

The DISNEY-CREATURES finish.

T

Ooh, let's get on the Teacups.

SCRAPPER

Excuse me? We're looking for the internet. Can you — wha-

They are shoved aboard the Teacups, which are office chairs covered in cardboard.
And they spin.

LOP

Hey Scrap, remember going to D-land?

SCRAPPER
(nope)

Sure.

LOR

Dad made us ride the oldest things first, like he was afraid
they were gonna yeet from under him. He'd point out - Look
how realistic that … dead hologram thing is. Can't beat old
Technology. And Mom would say,

(VOICE)

"Are you tired Bucko?"

LOR

Mom?

> LOR and SCAPPER's parents appear. Only
> these are kids with 2-D cardboard masks with
> pictures of a mom and dad.
> Maybe we've transported to that moment, like
> we're inside LOR's brain experiencing this
> memory.
> It feels like we're outside of time.
> Or maybe we just think we're being transported
> to LOR's memory.
> Maybe this is how Sad Disneyland works — they
> have people who pretend to be parents to more
> fully immerse in the nostalgia for what's lost.

MOM

Are you tired?

LOR

No, mom.

MOM

Hey look, bucko. Who's that?

LOR

Goofy.

DAD

When I was your age, I loved the Jungle River -

MOM

Jungle Cruise.
(they are inside the ride)
Keep your hands inside the ride at all times

LOR

I will mom.

DAD

They changed it again. Space Mountain's gone, too. Same as
the submarines. Oh you would have *loved* Cartopia - go-
carts with lawnmower engines. When I came here with your
grandparents, that was the thing to do. Drive hours in an un-
air-conditioned Chevy, smoggy LA traffic, your Grandpa
grumpy, my brother, your uncle, poking me - the first thing
I'd force 'em to do was jump into a go-cart. Just wanted to
pretend to be grown up.

MOM

Things change, dear.

DAD

Someday, you'll come here with your kids and talk about
what used to be.

> *MOM and DAD disappear.*
> *We hear and see:*
> *The intro to a parade!*
> *The floats are lit up with twinkle lights.*
> *It's candy and electric and weird and exciting.*
> *And then: a whistle.*

The DISNEYCREATURES freeze.
They begin to disrobe from their costumes,
trading them with uncostumed members of the
ensemble.
The "CHILD" takes the head from a creature.
This cast member under the mask... It's Mr.
AVERS —

                              T
Mr. Avers!

                         SCRAPPER
Small world.

                           LOR
Shut up.

                        Mr. AVERS
Who's that I hear? Is that —

                           LOR
We're over here.

              Mr. AVERS is blind now.

                        Mr. AVERS
              Is that - I hear Lorenzo, T, Scrapper.

                         SCRAPPER
Good to see you.

                        Mr. AVERS
Mr Avers would give his right kidney to could say the same.
Oh, I thought the firestarters got you. If I still had tear ducts
they'd be a leaking hard core. But I don't.

SCRAPPER

We thought you were dead.

Mr. AVERS

Takes a lot to kill Mr. Avers.

T

I'm sorry about your eyes.

Mr. AVERS

I saw a lot in my twenty years. A lot of ugly, and some pretty
stuff too.
It's beautiful isn't it? Un-Disneylandia.

SCRAPPER

It's sad, actually.

LOR

Scrap.

Mr. AVERS

We trade off being the enchanted kids, being the attractions.
I get so many hugs. People like to hug here, you know.

SCRAPPER

Mr. Avers. We can't stay. We need to find internet and this
place is creepy.

Mr. AVERS

Aw, I really wish you would, boogers.

T

Come with us.

Mr. AVERS

This is the end of Mr. Avers' story. Mr. Avers has always been a traveler. Wanted to be an astronaut. Stand on the moon and look out. The closest he'll get is Star Tours. And that's fine, that's fine. Because astronauts are so alone. They don't get so many hugs.

But you've been wandering blind now, too, I suppose. Perhaps wise Mr. Avers can be your eyes.

Mr. AVERS hands them his notebook.

SCRAPPER

The new Eden.

Mr. AVERS

They say a hundred thousand kids live there. It's self-sustaining. Safe journey, my friends.

In the meantime, you must excuse me. I'm late for the Country Bear Jamboree.

LOR
(reading)

It's in Canada.

Mr. AVERS leaves singing something Disney-like.

FOUR - Hometown Road

The CREW is in a new place. Suburbs. Stark and empty.

T

Hey fam.

New Eden — New Eden is hard to get to.

The path zigs and zags across the country.

And the trail takes us close to the brothers' hometown of Mantequilla.

SCRAPPER

And Lor forces us to take a side trip.

SHANE

You grew up in suburbia.

SCRAPPER and LOR

Shut up.

SHANE

I mean. It's nice, but —

COLLIN

Shane. Zip it. Zip.

SHANE

Where is everyone?

T

The city is… not bad. More whole than most. But… a ghost town.

COLLIN
Low humidity. Not a lot of green to take over.

LOR
We weren't really known for weather.

T
Lawns are dead, and there's paint peeling off of everything,
but it's intact.
Why isn't anyone around?

LOR
HELLO!

SCRAPPER
Okay, we're here. We've seen it.

LOR
We haven't even been home.
Scrap, you've wanted to visit.

SHANE
I'm going to look around.

SHANE exits.

T
We find Lor and Scrap's childhood home.
There's a key under the mat.
And we enter…

As they step in the house.

SCRAPPER
Oh no.

                    LOR

Mold.

                    They put on masks and turn on flashlights.

                    T

There's a table set.

                    We see the table.
                    And yes, it's set.

                    The sink's water is still running.

                    SCRAPPER

Don't sit down. Don't.

                    COLLIN

I wasn't.

                    SCRAPPER

This is where they were.
When they — on Day Zero.
She was here.
At the counter — washing dishes. See.
And he was eating breakfast.

                    LOR

Scrap - Dad did the dishes, not Mom.

                    T

So he left the water running.

                    LOR

Didn't even turn it off.

SCRAPPER

Don't —

But LOR turns it off.

SCRAPPER

I said don't.

SCRAPPER exits suddenly. He's upset.

LOR

They went with their clothes, you know. Funny. We didn't
have piles of clothes and pacemakers and hearing aids and
wedding rings and eyeglasses and wallets to hold on to —
little talismans that would say, yes, someone was here.

The floor quakes.
A beat to realize —

COLLIN

Yo. Exit. PRONTO.

LOR

Scrapper!

SCRAPPER

No!

LOR

Scapper.
The floor is.. not good.
Calmly walk to the exit. Now.
Our home is not safe.

We go outside.

> *They take off their masks.*
> *SCRAPPER follows.*

SCRAPPER

There's nothing left. Every picture is covered in mold,
Grandpa's art, everything is gone.

> *SHANE joins them.*

SHANE

City is deserted. You sure this wasn't a retirement
community?

LOR

Do we look retired?

COLLIN

That may have something to do with it.

> *COLLIN points. The others squint to see.*
> *T takes out the Geiger Counter.*

SHANE

A nuke plant, huh?

LOR

Clean power. Sort of.

SCRAPPER

That's a bad thing.
We should go.
Hey.
We should just go.
We need to - GAH.

>   *SCRAPPER is overwhelmed.*

LOR

Um, can you give us some privacy?

>   *The others shrug and turn away and cover their ears.*

LOR

Scrapper.

SCRAPPER

Let's just go.

LOR

Scrap.

SCRAPPER

Lor, I miss them so hard sometimes I can't breathe.
But I can't remember what they looked like.
I can't remember what Mom and Dad looked like.
Like, I think I think I picture them when I close my eyes, but
then I realize that the voice in my head belongs to Bolton's
sister, not Mom, that instead of Dad, I'm seeing Diesel -
remember him? - and instead of Grandpa, I'm imagining
Adam dressed as Santa.
They left us, Lor.
They left us.

SCRAPPER (CONT)

They left us.
                    (crying)
They left us
They left us.
They left us.
They left us.
They left us they left us they left us
And you're gonna leave. And then I'll be alone —
And I I I I

> *SCRAPPER is having a panic attack and can't breathe.*

> *SHANE turns.*

LOR

Go away.

SHANE

Breathe with me, breathe with me, kiddo - inhale, exhale
inhale,
exhale
2, 3.

> *SCRAPPER calms.*

SCRAPPER

Thank you.

LOR

Yeah. Thank you.

> *SHANE covers his ears.*
> *SCRAPPER vomits.*

LOR

Okay, there.
Um.
I uh
I don't know what to say - I don't -

> *LOR digs into his bag.*
> *He takes out the MAMA wig from earlier.*

LOR

Maybe Mom does.

SCRAPPER

Not funny.

LOR

Um.
"I'll love you forever
I'll love you for always…"
Scrap.
Kevin.
You look like Mom, okay? I look like Dad, you look like
Mom.
And —

> *SCRAPPER suddenly hugs LOR.*

SCRAPPER

Don't go anywhere.

LOR

I won't. I promise, okay.

A beat, then — we hear a gunshot. The crew scrambles for cover.

LOR

Hey? Don't shoot at us. We're having a moment.

T

What if it's a zombie?

SHANE

A zombie with guns?

VOICE

Greetings, looters.

SCRAPPER

Not looting. It's our home.

VOICE

I disagree. Everything Mantequilla's fallout touches belongs to me, and seeing as how I got a shotgun pointed at you, what I say is truth.

LOR

We're not looking for trouble.

VOICE

Lorenzo?

LOR

Yeah?

SCRAPPER

Who asks?

                    VOICE
Kevin? Is that you?

                    SCRAPPER
I kinda go by Scrapper now.

                    VOICE
That a nickname?

                    SCRAPPER
Obviously.

                    VOICE
I thought you fell out of the sky.

                    LOR
The hurricane grounded us.

                    COLLIN
And I'm Collin, and this is Shane.

                    T
They're dating.

                    SHANE
He doesn't need to know that.

                    T
Call me T.

                    COLLIN
Burning a lot of hourglass sand with jabber.

VOICE

Guess who I am, Lorenzo? Here's a clue: I WANT TO PLAY
BOWSER, BUTTHEAD!

LOR

YOU ALWAYS PLAY BOWSER, DORKWARD, YOU
MAKE ME PLAY PRINCESS PEACH!

VOICE

YOU'RE GOOD AT PRINCESS PEACH!

CHRIS enters. He carries a sack and shotgun.
He is in a business suit.

LOR

DORKWAD!

CHRIS

BUTTHEAD. So, the Ramos sibs have returned to
Mantequilla! Bienvenidos.
Man, Kevin. Look at you.

LOR

He went through puberty.

SCRAPPER

Thank you, Lor.

CHRIS

Man, nothing changes you so much as puberty and the
apocalypse.

SCRAPPER

We're not staying long.

CHRIS

Man, you HAVE to join my family for dinner.
                    (indicating the sack)
It's fresh.
You can meet my wife — and the kids—

LOR

What?

CHRIS

Here's my business card. It's the big house on the corner.
You can't miss it.
You're all invited. Man, this is gonna be dope.

         CHRIS exits.

                    T

He made the Geiger Counter ping.

LOR

I guess - we're going to dinner?
You okay with that?

SCRAPPER

Sure. Yeah.
I need to get cleaned up.

SHANE

I think I'll pass.

COLLIN

Same.

         *The group exist, but COLLIN pulls SHANE
         aside.*

116

COLLIN

Whatcha take, Shane?

SHANE

Nothing.

COLLIN

Shane. I know you.

SHANE pulls it out. A ring.

COLLIN

Looter.

This becomes something of a proposal.

COLLIN

No. Gross. Ew.

SHANE

For you.

COLLIN

I can't take it. Nope nope nope.

SHANE

I like you, Collin Beck. And I want to marry you sort-of.
It can be a temporary thing, like we're married for a little
while.

COLLIN

That ring belonged to someone, and when we get them back,
they're gonna miss it.

SHANE

No one cares.

COLLIN

I care.
Look I'll take a can from a stranger's cupboard. Borrow
batteries smashed out of Wal-Mart. I can't take something
that someone loved and touched and thought was special.

SHANE

Collin can't stand imaginary folks disliking him.

COLLIN

Nope nope. Never have.

SHANE

I'll return it.

COLLIN

Good.

SHANE

And... what about my question?

COLLIN

If we were normal, and the world were normal, we'd break
up you know, sooner or later. Mistakes.

SHANE

We're good at making them.
Collin, the world is not normal.
So... we get to invent things. Like — I think we'd get back
together. Eventually.

                    COLLIN
A few years down the line.
We meet at a conference -

                    SHANE
At a protest.

                    COLLIN
And you're be recently single. And we hit it off.

                    SHANE
Marriage. Two kids.

                    COLLIN
We get older. You'll get a job repairing ice caps.

                    SHANE
You'll be a musician.

                    COLLIN
You'll have a cancer scare at 55.

                    SHANE
But we'll be around into our 80s. Which one of us will go
first?

                    COLLIN
I will.

                    SHANE
Hey.
When they come back.
When we bring them back.
We'll return the ring.
I promise.

SHANE (CONT)

Please.

COLLIN takes the ring.

COLLIN

Okay.

A gentle transition to:

T

Dinner at Chris's place.
It's a mansion. One of those houses that feel like it ate another house.
And it's full - pool tables, grand piano, layers of rugs, chandeliers, a stuffed boar —

They are at dinner.

CHRIS

Everyone fled when they thought the nuke plant would go.
The alarms blared for months.
No one was there to tell it to stop, it's cool, no meltdown.
Man, it was a pain in my you-know-what, but I eventually shot enough of them out to have some quiet.
          (indicating a makeshift thing memorial)
Look, I made this for you see?

LOR

A memorial.

CHRIS

For you. I wanted to honor you, cuz.

                              LOR
"The Buttwads"

                              CHRIS
Have some more wine.
So, I've been in Beverly McMansion for about three years.
My place burned down, but then I realized, I could have any
house I wanted, and any thing I wanted from any house. I
wasn't materialistic, but then I got me some materials, and
let me tell you. Wood floors. Portico. Man, that stuff
CHANGES you. You find a boat and you're like, who's boat
is this boat, and then you're like, this boat is MY boat. Nice.

                              LOR
You mentioned —

                              CHRIS
The Boomers, Gen X, they had it all, and they mortgaged
our future to buy it, and look what they built with it. Look.
We were all set to scuffle for scraps, but when they cleared
away, man, we got it all.

                               T
So much.

                              CHRIS
It's amazing. Bam. Lorenzo, Kevin, other one - you gotta see
the game room, did I show you the game room?

                            SCRAPPER
Twice.

                              LOR
You said we had family, Chris?

CHRIS

I did? I did!
Right, right.
Now, don't freak out.
Let me introduce you to my wife? Carol. Carol. This is
Lorenzo. This is Kevin. They are my cousins.

It's a mannequin.

CHRIS

The wedding was lit.

LOR

Um.

CHRIS

Oh, and let me show you the kids.

They are also items.

SCRAPPER

Dude.

CHRIS

Don't be like that.

SCRAPPER

Lor, does this run in the family?

CHRIS

I know what this looks like.
I was really alone, you know.
Everyone else left. I made do.

                    LOR

Chris, you should join us.

                   CHRIS

I like my life.

                    LOR

You live next to a nuclear power plant.

                   CHRIS

That fuels my X-Box.

                    LOR

I don't even know what we're eating, but I suspect that it
was once domesticated.

                   CHRIS

Cows were domesticated, too.

                    LOR

We're your family.

                   CHRIS

You could stay here. It's comfortable.

                  SCRAPPER

Lor. I'm not staying. I'm not, okay? Lor, I can't, we need to -

                    LOR

Chris.
Thank you for you offer.
We really can't, cousin Dorkwad.

                  SCRAPPER

We've got things to do.

LOR

You sure we can't convince you to join us?

CHRIS

I like my life, Buttwad.

Look around. Okay, nuke plant, whatever. But at least I don't have to commute.

I live in suburbia! I live in a MANSION! I own a piece of the pinnacle of human civilization.

I got my spouse. I got my garden. I got my kids. I got an extensive record collection, and a college degree - a college that I started! I have accomplishments! What more could I ask for?

Lorenzo! I have achieved the American dream.

What more can a man ask for?

FIVE - Broadway Bound

T

Update:
According to the maps, we have to go the long way around
New Jersey. And we can't help but want to stop and see —
the self-declared cultural capital of the world. New York,
New York

SCRAPPER

So nice they named it twice.

T

We explore Manhattan by boat.
The streets have ruptured. Subways flooded and collapsed,
sewers are ripped open, rivers criss-cross places that tourists

SCRAPPER

like us

T

used to capture in photographs

SCRAPPER

like PokemonGo.

T

Why was this stuff famous?

LOR

5th Avenue

SCRAPPER

Shopping

Christopher Street

Gay District

Wall Street.

SHANE, LOR, and SCRAPPER

Protestors.

T

In the windows of the buildings, we see candles. There are
some holds-outs who live in a city that meant so much, that
took so much —
Times Square is quiet.
We dock on the shore of Central Park.
Grass is growing in the tears of concrete. The Park is
pushing past cement borders meant to keep it out of
midtown. It seems to be swallowing Manhattan.

SCRAPPER

Look.

T

There are lights

COLLIN

It's a Broadway house.

T

I want to see —

126

COLLIN

Let's go. I've always wanted to see a Broadway show.

T

We go inside the hollow of the theatre. And we see:

> *A weird performance from a musical.*
> *It's terrible. And wonderful.*
> *Made by theatre kids who once upon a time*
> *dreamed of being on Broadway[4].*

SHANE

Goes to show even the apocalypse can't kill musical theatre.

T

Nope.

LOR

Really no.

SCRAPPER

I liked it.

COLLIN

When every human has shuffled off this mortal coil, I guarantee there will still be mice and cockroaches skittering over the boards in Broadway singing *Phantom*.

---

[4] We did this quite simply: parodying *Phantom of the Opera,* with the Phantom yelling "Sing! Keep singing! That's good, keep going!" while two of our actors played Christine hitting the high notes. You may pick any Broadway musical you want to parody a moment from.

SIX - Crossing Over

The group is resting. They've set up camp on the
border between Canada and the US.
(There could even be a sign that says "Now
entering Canada" that they're resting under.)
SHANE takes T's phone, and hops back and
forth between the countries.
This is a quieter moment.

SHANE

Watch me.

COLLIN

US.
Canada.
US.
Canada.
US.
Canada.

SHANE

Past
… Present.
Past —

COLLIN

Not future?

SHANE

Sure. Future.
Of course.
Future.

A kiss? a handhold?

Let this moment linger. Let this moment be a
secret conversation between two lovers.
So, it's a bit dorky.
And it's time to go to sleep like everyone else.

COLLIN

Look.

SHANE

Where?

COLLIN

Up.

SHANE

Shooting star! Make a wish.

COLLIN

No. Satellite. A bit of the past skittering across the sky.

SHANE

It's the future.

SHANE sleeps.

A blink.

Then it's morning.

COLLIN is gone.

SHANE

Collin.
Collin?
Collin Beck?
        (frantic search, frantic search, frantic search)

                    SHANE (CONT)
COLLIN BECK!
Where are you?

                    The others awaken.

                    SCRAPPER
What's going on?

                    SHANE
Collin's disappeared.

                    SCRAPPER
The aliens got him. They knew — so they disappeared him.

                    SHANE
COLLIN BECK!

                         T
No.

                    T finds an envelope.
                    The ring is on it.

                         T
A letter.
                    (meaning the missing adults)
They never left things behind.

                    SCRAPPER
Don't —

                    T opens the letter. There's an ID in it, along with
                    a note.

SCRAPPER

What's that?
What's that?

T
(reading, realizing)
Collin Beck was 19. He had a fake ID.

SCRAPPER leaves suddenly.

LOR

Scrapper, Scrapper!

LOR follows.

T
He needs to work out his feelings.

SHANE

What's the note say?

T
"I only wanted people to like me. Then they did.
I sort of believed it myself.
I'm sorry."
Shane, I'm sorry. Do you want —

T indicates: the ring Collin gave you?

SHANE

No.
No.

A sudden yell from offstage.

131

T

What's that?

> *The yell goes on. It's a wailing on physical pain.*
> *Then LOR limps on, bloody and wheezing.*
> *SCRAPPER helps.*

SCRAPPER

A trap. There was a trap.

LOR

Aaaaah!

SCRAPPER

Breathe, Lor. Shane- something to wrap the wound.

> *LOR grimaces in pain and starts to*
> *hyperventilate.*

T

It's deep, Scrap.

SHANE

What kind of trap, Scrapper? A person trap —

T

Shane.
Uh, Shane!
It was them —

> *We see them now.*
> *Looming over our crew.*
> *FIRESTARTERS.*

T

So many of them.

SCRAPPER

You gonna join them Shane?

T

Don't joke —

SCRAPPER

I'm not.
Are you, Shane?

>*SHANE is paralyzed.*
>*Is SHANE going to join them?*
>*Then.*

SHANE

Let us go in peace.
Please.
My heart was just broken, so if you want —

>*The FIRESTARTERS point at T's phone.*
>*The FIRESTARTERS begin to stomp.*
>*Hesitating at first, T offers her phone.*
>*A FIRESTARTER breaks it.*
>*A beat.*
>*The FIRESTARTERS exit.*

SCRAPPER

Shane?

>*SHANE does not follow the exiting*
>*FIRESTARTERS.*
>*SHANE lifts LOR.*

SHANE
Come on.

T picks up her phone.

SEVEN - New Eden

An empty forest. Snow on the ground.
The crew enters.
LOR is on improvised crutches, and is suffering
from the injury.
T takes out her shattered phone.

T

Winter. Oh. Canada.
Hey… fam-of-futuro.
The hopeful.
The…
Um.

SCRAPPER

Put that crap away —

T

Hey.

LOR

It's broken, Scrap.

T

Maybe it's working and I can't tell? Maybe?
We have to document this.

SCRAPPER

Give it, then.
(SCRAPPER takes it.)
What's up, fam-squad. Here's the moral of this story coming
at you:
Everyone lies.
Even Mr. Avers.

                              LOR
No. Not him.

                               T
According to the map, it's here.

                           SCRAPPER
According to the map, according to the map — DO YOU
SEE ANYTHING?? DO YOU?? I see trees, that's what I
see. Maybe they live in the trees. Maybe they're bugs.

                            SHANE
Leave her alone.

            SCRAPPER howls.

                              LOR
I don't have energy for this.

                               T
There's — a few burned out buildings.

                            SHANE
Look.

            SHANE lifts up a sign
            It's an advert for soda, with Santa Claus.
            Only Santa is spray painted out.

                              LOR
I got one too.

            Something else where there's a brilliant X in
            front of the 'adult'

SHANE

Firestarters.

SCRAPPER

Friends of yours.

SHANE

Dude.

T

It *was* here. Mr. Avers didn't lie.

LOR

What's it matter?

T

It matters. IT MATTERS!

SHANE

Keep it down. They could still be around.

Instant quiet-ish

SCRAPPER

What happened to the people?

LOR

I don't want to think about it.

SCRAPPER

I don't see graves.

SHANE

If there isn't someone to bury them, you wouldn't see
graves.

SCRAPPER

I don't see bodies.

LOR

Scavengers. Woods are full of them.
This is our Eden, folks.
A burned warehouse.
Cast out by vengeful self-appointed Gods trying to flood the
world -

SHANE

You're mixing up the stories.

LOR

Am I?
…
Good thing we took our time getting here.
And it's starting to snow.
Is that a moose?

****

Time passes.

****

T

Update
To my imaginary…
To me.
Um.
We're pretty far north.

T (CONT)

I think we're lost.

LOR

They went with their clothes. Isn't that funny? Wherever
they are, they're still wearing underwear.

SHANE

Lor?

LOR

Just in case.
I want you to bury me in my favorite shirt. The Metallica
one.
I suppose you should keep this watch, though I do feel naked
without it.

SCRAPPER

Lor.

T

You sound weird.

LOR

I'm fine.
I just.
Really wish
Really really wish

>   *LOR collapses.*
>   *SHANE catches him.*

SCRAPPER

Lor!

                              LOR
Shhh.
Firestarters around. All around, look at them. You see them?
They want to —

                             SHANE
Lor, keep things in focus.

                             SHANE
Get a fire going. We'll keep him warm. Um.

                            SCRAPPER
Help!

            This terrifies T.

                               T
No, keep it down, keep it down.

                             SHANE
Lor? Please. Please.

                            SCRAPPER
HEEEEELP!
HEEEEEEEEEELP!!

                               T
Shhh shhh shhh!

                            SCRAPPER
HELP HELP HELP HELP!

                               T
You need a time-out!

Then -
We hear something.
It's an engine.

                    SCRAPPER

What's that?

          T pulls out SHANE's weapon.

                         T

Not worth the risk.

                    (VOICE)

Ho ho ho.

                         T

Identify yourself!

          The weapon goes off.

                    (VOICE)

Hey!

                         T

Sorry, I'm really clumsy.

                    (VOICE)
Are you in need of medical assistance?

                    SCRAPPER
That's what "help" means!

                    (VOICE)
Put the weapon away, and we can help.

T

Are you a firestarter?

(VOICE)

Oh yeah, no, 'fraid not, sorry.
If you put your weapon down, I can help.
I have A LOT of First AID badges. I'm a Junior EMT. I'm
wicked good.

> *JOHNNY enters. He's... dressed up in a sort of*
> *Santa Claus outfit / scrub hybrid.*

JOHNNY

Namaste. I'm your medical semi-professsional, Johnny B.
What do we have here?

SCRAPPER

Namaste. He's...

JOHNNY

Clearly in need of medical assistance.

T

You're dressed as Santa.

JOHNNY

It's that time of year.
Well, come on. Give him a lift.
We don't have all day.

T

(narrating)

We load Lor into his ... ambulance Range Rover thunder
car.

142

They do.
It's loud.

                    SHANE
This thing is like right out of Mad Max.

                    JOHNNY
I loved those movies.

                      T
Where are you taking us?

                    JOHNNY
Sorry, should have said. We're called New Eden.

                   SCRAPPER
We were just there?

                    JOHNNY
That was old Eden from when we were a start-up.

                      T
It burned down.

                    JOHNNY
Yeah.
We burned it down.

                     ALL
You?

JOHNNY

Oh yeah. To the ground.
It was a little too much like the old way. Oh, and with these
cameras, we monitor anyone who shows up looking.
Americans you know, you never know what you're getting
when you get an American.

SCRAPPER

Does New Eden have the internet?
T needs it.

JOHNNY

We got dialup.
We got other stuff, some you know. Antibiotics — we'll get
you patched up.

LOR

Stop stop.
Let me be.
I'm old. I don't matter.
I'm gonna disappear on you pretty soon.

JOHNNY

That doesn't matter.
Bring us your tired, your sick, your you know. You.

LOR

Yeah it does.
I'm a burden — just let me stop.
Oh.
Look at them all.

SCRAPPER

Who?

LOR

All of them.
Them.

SCRAPPER

What do you see?

LOR

I see
mom
I see
dad
I see them all.
Hey guys

SCRAPPER

Lor. LOR??

> *Time slows to a stop.*
> *SCRAPPER is sure LOR is dying. The crew is*
> *frozen in panic*
> *Except — LOR, who gets up and addresses the*
> *audience.*

LOR

They're sure caring for me, what with the little time I have.
They should be saving that for someone else.

T

This is one of those 'clap if you believe' moments... Where
time freezes and rules are broken.
> *(T pulls out the ring from earlier)*
Whose ring is this?

ADULT

It's mine.

T

Ah. An adult. You have a message for us?

>*This ring belongs to an audience member, an
>adult. You know, one of the missing.
>This adult is a surprise to the actors. Maybe a
>parent or a teacher or a friend or a grandparent.
>T hands the ring to The Adult.
>The Adult reads a letter, a message from the
>adults. Please see the POSTSCRIPT LETTER
>for more information.*

THE LETTER FROM THE ADULTS

Listen my dears, young ones. You are in so much pain in a
broken world. You are of age before you should be, and
though we say this from a distance, we now see you.

My dears. Go on.

What you have taught me is this: Life is clawing past yet
another disappointment, it's scratching at the dirt, and it's
even finding joy in the scratch. It's grabbing the hand that's
offered you, getting up, and grabbing who else fell down to
bring them up too.

Yes. We, the ones who came before you, are imperfect. And
we've passed many of our faults on to you, as you will to
yours. And if aliens came to visit, they'd see creatures
who... can think and know the fragility of life. Know the
scarring. Know our own imperfections. And yet they'd see -

146

THE LETTER FROM THE ADULTS (CONT)

We humans, we build, we build again, and the best is when we learn from those what fell before. We stare rejection in its teeth and we say, nah. I matter. From city rubble, we hear laughter and singing and we see grass that was called weeds once upon a time break through the cracks in sidewalks through sheer force of will.

We are stubborn, us human creatures.

This is what you've taught me, you know. You, the generation who saves each other.

So this is what I give you back: You are loved. Each and every one. Forever. Go on, my dears. Go on.

EPILOGUE-ISH

T

Hi.
T here.
And - my friends. We're broadcasting.
From Eden.
This is probably the last time you'll hear from me.
There are some things that we should let go.
It's March 1. 2026. Two weeks after Valentine's day.

> *LOR appears.*
> *He's limping, cane in hand.*
> *LOR and T's eyes meet.*

LOR

Say that again.

> *As T says the following, SCRAPPER enters,*
> *bringing LOR his inhaler.*

T

Six years and two weeks ago, every adult on the planet
disappeared. Day Zero. They left us with a ruptured ozone
and marine ice turning to water and hundreds of nuke plants
stewing themselves. And the kids took over. Some turned
inward. Some lived in sparkles of nostalgia. Some lived
stolen dreams. Some collected each other.
And now, it's March 1, 2026.

LOR

March 1, 2026.

And …

They haven't come back.

But they left us with each other. Which is a beautiful thing.

And they left us with the question: What do we do now?

LOR

Whatever we want.

> *T turns off the recording.*
> *She goes to a radio.*
> *She turns it on.*
> *It doesn't start.*
> *Then it does.*
> *Static.*
> *She touches it again.*
> *Then a little music*
> *What is that?*
> *Something you've heard before?*
> *Maybe it is. Maybe it isn't.*
> *She turns off the radio.*

END of PLAY

POSTSCRIPT LETTER

First, let me list the original cast. This play was originally written for and with a group of extraordinary teenagers at Skybridge Academy (now called Appamada School). The cast was the following:

Trinity Bobo ….. T
Nicholas Dussere …. Lor
Collin Beck ….. Scrapper (and Second Young Adult)
Jacob Gantenbein ….. Mr. Avers, Ensemble
Percy Young …… Shane
Griffin Wilson ….. Collin Beck and the Mean Math Dude
Torin Ginty ….. DJ, Brat, Sad Disneykid, Johnny B
Ethan Hennehoefer ….. Adam, Young Adult, Bootlicker, Dad, Chris
Ezra Wilson ….. Bolt, Citizen, Mom, Ensemble
Dorian "Zev" Kweller … Ozli, the Feral Child, Headmaster, Ensemble

Roman Harrison as the understudy
Claire Fischer as Propsmaster
Sam Penner as Master Carpenter
Griffin Wilson on Lighting Design
Ezra Wilson on Costume Design

And now, let's talk about time, and how to adjust the script to fit your moment.

In the fall of 2019, we were not predicting the subsequent pandemic; rather, this play was in response to a general feeling of anxiety about the world - the sense that *something catastrophic* was on its way, whether it was climate change or war or some other disaster - as well as a pushback against nihilism. The Disappearance does not metaphorically represent the pandemic, though I do think the pandemic does represent the kind of catastrophe we were dreading.

If you choose to leave the Disappearance Day in 2020, that's totally fine; you will draw comparisons to the pandemic, which is not inappropriate.

If you choose to update the day of the Disappearance, that is also great. Part of the fun for our cast has been to experience moving through the dates. This has kept the play with us.

And part of the fun in writing the play was identifying what was going on in pop culture that would be preserved. The song of the summer was clearly Old Town Road with a dash of Lizzo, and our gaming crew were digging into Fortnite.

So here's my recommendation: Early in the process, spend some time as a group identifying present cultural touchstones, list them out, and fold them into the play. You have my permission to update what needs to be updated. And to have fun.

So, let's talk about The Letter from the Adults.
This play culminates in a letter from the missing adults. When we staged it with my teenage actors, I asked the actors' parents to volunteer to read this letter. I asked that these volunteers keep their participation secret from their child, though the actors know the content of the letter. As the parent reads the letter, the cast comes out and listens. The sense of this moment being in the present was important to me. The roles between actor and audience are reversed. This moment also makes the play necessarily theatre.